LinkedIn® Sales Navigator

WITHDRAWN

for dummies®

A Wiley Brand

LinkedIn® Sales Navigator

by Perry van Beek
Founder, Social.ONE

LinkedIn® Sales Navigator For Dummies®

Published by: **John Wiley & Sons, Inc.,** 111 River Street, Hoboken, NJ 07030-5774, www.wiley.com

Copyright © 2018 by John Wiley & Sons, Inc., Hoboken, New Jersey

Published simultaneously in Canada

For general information on our other products and services, please contact our Customer Care Department within the U.S. at 877-762-2974, outside the U.S. at 317-572-3993, or fax 317-572-4002. For technical support, please visit www.wiley.com/techsupport.

Wiley publishes in a variety of print and electronic formats and by print-on-demand. Some material included with standard print versions of this book may not be included in e-books or in print-on-demand. If this book refers to media such as a CD or DVD that is not included in the version you purchased, you may download this material at http://booksupport.wiley.com. For more information about Wiley products, visit www.wiley.com.

Library of Congress Control Number: 2018949882

ISBN 978-1-119-42768-1 (pbk); ISBN 978-1-119-42775-9 (ebk); ISBN 978-1-119-42776-6 (ebk)

Manufactured in the United States of America

C10002852_072718

Contents at a Glance

Table of Contents

Introduction

Salespeople need leads. That's nothing new. What has changed though, is the way in which salespeople get new leads. In 1995, cold-calling was hot, no pun intended. You just bought yourself a list of leads and started calling everyone on that list. Or you ripped a few pages out of the telephone directory in your hotel room and started knocking on doors. That's something I used to do — successfully, too!

Would that still work today? Of course not! For starters, there are no telephone directories in hotel rooms anymore. I suppose you could go online to find and print a list of leads and then start knocking on doors. But if you can go online, so can your buyers. And they do!

Your buyers are not just relying on Google to find what they are looking for, either. In fact, a 2014 study by IBM revealed that 75 percent of customers use social media as part of their buying process (www.nancypekala.com/wp-content/uploads/2012/06/ibm-social-selling.pdf). An even bigger challenge for salespeople is that according to a study by HubSpot, only 29 percent of people want to talk to a salesperson to learn more about a product or service, while 62 percent will consult a search engine (www.hubspot.com/marketing-statistics).

This is why many salespeople rank prospecting as one of the most difficult parts of the sales process.

LinkedIn recognized this rapid change in the world of sales and introduced Sales Navigator in 2012 to help salespeople with their social-selling efforts. LinkedIn Sales Navigator is a premium subscription service designed to help salespeople identify, follow, and connect with decision-makers. At the time, it was still part of the main LinkedIn professional networking site. In 2014, around the time LinkedIn attained 300 million users, LinkedIn Sales Navigator was introduced as a stand-alone tool.

About This Book

LinkedIn Sales Navigator For Dummies is your comprehensive guide to using Sales Navigator for social selling on LinkedIn. I introduce you to all the features of LinkedIn Sales Navigator and even show you how to sign up, if you haven't done that already. This book is useful whether you're just starting out with social selling or you're an experienced social seller already. In addition to showing you how to map the buyer's journey, identify and connect with leads, and become top-of-mind with your leads, it addresses what techniques are effective on LinkedIn Sales Navigator, helping you determine your own successful social-selling strategy.

How This Book Is Organized

This book is divided into the following five parts:

Part 1: Getting Ready to Generate Leads

In this part of the book I show you how to plan your roadmap for social-selling success and identify your ideal buying personas. I start our journey by taking a deeper look at the definition of social selling and how social selling can help you increase your sales results.

Part 2: Building a Database of Leads

In the previous part, you identified your ideal buying personas. Now that you know who to look for, in this part 1 show you how to find them with Sales Navigator. I also show you how to save your searches, leads, and accounts.

Part 3: Engaging with Leads

You've now added a bunch of leads and accounts. Now what? Well, these people you are now following may not even know that you exist. In this part, we look at how you can get on their radar in a non-pushy manner. In this part 1 also show you how to reach out to your leads using connection requests and InMail messages.

Part 4: Turning Leads into Valuable Relationships

Fifty percent of identified sales leads are still not ready to buy. One of the first sales lessons I learned was that when a potential client says "no," he or she usually means "not now." Therefore, it's important that when potential clients say no, you don't just forget about them and move on to the next. In this part 1 show you how to encourage the people you're following to think of you first when they're ready to buy.

Part 5: The Part of Tens

This is one of my favorite parts, as I get to share some advanced strategies here. For starters, I share ten tips for advanced lead generation within Sales Navigator. These tips will work best for you if you've already read the first four parts of this book and you're comfortable using Sales Navigator. I also include ten tips on how to make the most out of managing your accounts.

There are many people who inspire me in the LinkedIn and social-selling world. So, in this part, I include a list of ten people who I believe you should also follow, as their content is highly valuable. And for the readers who just cannot get enough, I also include ten additional resources you may want to consult to up your social-selling game. Some are free, some are not, but all are excellent!

Foolish Assumptions

In writing this book I assume that you:

>> Are a sales professional familiar with LinkedIn with an established LinkedIn network.

>> Recognize that social networking — and social selling — is becoming more and more prevalent among your businesses and your customers.

>> Either have a Sales Navigator account or plan on signing up for one.

Icons Used in This Book

Throughout this book you'll find special icons that call your attention to important information. Here's what to expect:

TIP

This icon is used for (more) helpful suggestions and additional tidbits of information you may find useful.

REMEMBER

Everything is worth remembering in this book, but this icon points out the specific information that bears repeating.

WARNING

This icon is used when you should heed my advice to avoid potential pitfalls.

Where to Go from Here

If you don't know where you're going, Chapter 1 is a good place to start. However, if you see a particular topic that piques your interest, feel free to jump ahead to that chapter. Each chapter is written to stand on its own, so you can start reading anywhere in the book and skip around as you see fit.

This book also comes with a free Social Selling Strategy Cheat Sheet that gives you seven quick strategies on how to quickly and efficiently optimize your social-selling game plan. To get this Cheat Sheet, simply go to www.dummies.com and search for *LinkedIn Sales Navigator For Dummies Cheat Sheet* in the Search box.

Now, go get you social-selling game on! I wish you the very best.

1
Getting Ready to Generate Leads

Chapter **1**

Selling Is a Social Business

S ocial media has been around for over a decade, and social media marketing isn't that much younger. It's only been in the past five years or so that sales professionals have really harnessed the power of social media to connect with prospects and close the deal.

In this chapter, I discuss what social selling is and what goes into a successful social-selling endeavor. I also introduce you to a powerful tool, LinkedIn Sales Navigator, and tell you about two of its especially robust features — the Social Selling Index and TeamLink — that will help you take your social selling to the next level.

Defining Social Selling

What is *social selling* exactly? It's pretty much just what the name sounds like — utilizing online social channels for selling purposes. Sales professionals interact with prospective customers through social media by answering questions and providing helpful content in order to move the potential customer through the sales funnel.

When it comes to having a successful social-selling strategy in your organization, you need to know right from the start that social selling is about both outbound prospecting and inbound marketing:

>> **Outbound prospecting:** involves gathering intelligence and learning as much as possible about your customer base.

>> **Inbound marketing:** is the process of building a pipeline of leads by providing content, such as in the form of newsletters, blogs, and postings on social media platforms.

Most sales teams are already using tools like LinkedIn and Twitter to learn about their customer bases. It's the process of building an inbound marketing system, however, that's the hard part. That's because the process of discovering, curating, and sharing content can take significant time from someone's day. This is why LinkedIn Sales Navigator is such a game changer. It gives you the ability to do both outbound prospecting and inbound marketing all on one platform.

Looking at the Four Pillars of Social Selling

According to LinkedIn, social selling involves taking a four-pronged approach that it dubbed the "four pillars of social selling." These four pillars are defined as follows:

>> **Create a professional brand.** Having a strong professional brand shows prospects that your company is active in all areas of the industry. Customers only do business with brands they trust.

>> **Focus on the right prospects.** LinkedIn states that over 76 percent of buyers are open to having a conversation with a sales professional via social media. Sales Navigator helps you identify the right decision-maker with whom to have this conversation through the use of filters and advanced search functions.

>> **Engage with insights.** Position yourself as a subject matter expert and thought leader by sharing helpful industry news as well as commenting on posts made by others. This helps salespeople remain in potential clients' minds.

>> **Build trusted relationships.** Establish a rapport with prospects by identifying a common ground. Provide relevant content that addresses their pain points as opposed to some generic sales materials that try to cover every feature of your product.

Collecting, Connecting, Converting: The Formula for Success

Collecting, connecting, and converting are often called the "three C's of online sales" (see Figure 1-1). However, they are the key ingredients to the recipe of any type of sales, not just the online variety. If you were speaking with someone who knew nothing at all about sales, and you say that all it comes down to are those three words, they'd know exactly what to do to make a sale (in theory, of course). Here's a refresher to set the stage:

>> **Collecting:** This is how a business gathers its intel about contacts and leads. The methodology used differs depending on the organization and where the potential customer is in the buying cycle, but collecting generally includes things like capturing email addresses via landing pages, webinar sign-ups, and opt-in forms. It's best to try out different collection methods to ensure you're using the best one for your needs.

>> **Connecting:** Here's where an organization makes the first contact with the prospective customer, be it through automated response email or other personalized follow-up sequences. It's important that the connection method used is specific to the recipient. It must speak to the buyer's needs at the precise time and location in the buyer's journey to bring the recipient closer to the sale. (Chapter 3 is dedicated to the buyer's journey.)

>> **Converting:** Now we get to enjoy the fruits of our labors. Converting is when the *potential* customer becomes an *actual* customer, or at least becomes a well-qualified lead. The point is that the customer took a direct step further along the buyer's journey, be it scheduling a demo or making an actual purchase.

The three C's may seem overwhelming or maybe even like a waste of time. You may even be tempted to skip a step or two. But never fear! LinkedIn created a helpful, robust sales tool that helps professionals move through those stages (hopefully) without a hitch. It's what we all came here for. It's LinkedIn Sales Navigator, and it's time we jumped right into it!

Exploring the Sales Navigator Plans

As of this writing, LinkedIn offers everyone a free month to try LinkedIn Sales Navigator. After that, LinkedIn offers three Sales Navigator plans: Professional, Team, and Enterprise. Each plan comes with specific benefits:

» **Professional:** $79.99 per month (billed monthly) or $779.88 per year (which breaks down to $64.99 per month) when you buy an annual subscription. This account includes the following features:

- 20 InMail messages per month

- 1,500 saved leads

- Who's viewed your profile

- Extended LinkedIn network access

- Advanced lead and company search

- Lead and account recommendations

- Territory preferences

- Job change alerts

- Prospect and company news alerts

- Sales Navigator for Gmail

- Notes and tags
- Learning center
- Sales Navigator Mobile App

>> **Team:** $129.99 per month (billed monthly) or $1,199.88 per year (which breaks down to $99.99 per month) when you buy an annual subscription. This account includes everything in the Professional-level plan plus the following features (the benefits marked with double asterisks [**] are only available for accounts with ten or more team members):

- Search includes people who follow your company page
- 10 additional InMail messages per month
- 3,500 additional saved leads (5,000 total)
- 10 PointDrive presentations per month
- Team network warm introductions with TeamLink Extend
- CRM (customer relationship management) integrations
- 25 out-of-network unlocks per month
- Basic seat management
- Usage reporting
- Volume and multi-year discounts**
- Invoicing**
- A dedicated relationship manager**

>> **Enterprise:** Pricing depends on the needs of your organization so you must call for specific pricing information. This account includes everything in the Professional- and Team-level plans in addition to the following features:

- 20 additional InMail messages per month
- 5,000 additional saved leads (10,000 total)
- Unlimited PointDrive presentations per month
- Company network warm introductions with TeamLink Extend
- Single sign-on integrations
- Enterprise-grade seat management

Activating Your Sales Navigator Account

Now that we've gone through the nitty-gritty about what each subscription plan offers, it's time to sign up! You can begin your journey into LinkedIn Sales Navigator–land directly from your personal LinkedIn account.

Once you're logged into your LinkedIn account from a desktop computer, follow these steps to activate a Sales Navigator account:

1. **Click the Work (or More) icon in the main navigation menu bar at the top of your screen, as shown in Figure 1-2.**

    This icon looks like a grid with six squares. A drop-down menu appears.

2. **Select the Sales Solutions option.**

    You are now on the Sales Navigator home page as shown in Figure 1-3.

Click to access Sales Navigator

FIGURE 1-2: Click the Work icon to access Sales Navigator.

REMEMBER

This set of steps assumes you're ready to purchase a Sales Navigator plan. If you're still trying to decide if the service is right for you, you can either request a demo or sign up for a free trial (individual accounts only) by following Steps 1 and 2 and then selecting either the Request Free Demo or Start Your Free Trial button and following the on-screen prompts. If you are ready to purchase a plan, continue to Step 3.

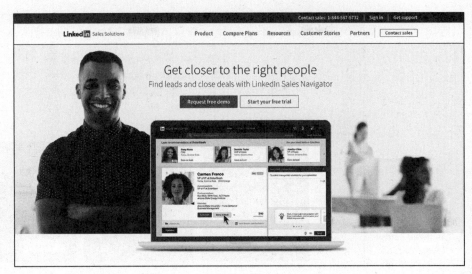

FIGURE 1-3:
Your introduction to Sales Navigator.

3. **Click Compare Plans in the top menu bar.**

   You see the subscription plan options shown in Figure 1-4.

4. **In the subscription box of choice, click the Buy Now button.**

   If you're buying a subscription for yourself or a small team, select the Professional-level plan. If you're making the purchase for a team of two to ten people, you may select the Team option; although, some of the benefits of the Team-level plan (such as PointDrive) only become available when ten or more licences are purchased directly from LinkedIn (not online). With a team over ten people you also have the option to select an Enterprise-level plan, and you must also call to speak with a LinkedIn Sales Navigator sales representative. The remainder of these steps take you through the process to purchase a Professional-level plan.

   You can purchase a plan at an annual rate and save up to 25 percent on the monthly cost, or you can choose the convenience of a monthly subscription and pay a little bit more.

REMEMBER

5. **On the page that appears, click the Select Plan button in the purple highlighted box (Figure 1-5).**

   At this point the page slides down and you're *finally* presented with a button to click to actually sign up for the service! You never thought we'd get there, huh? Well, we made it . . . almost.

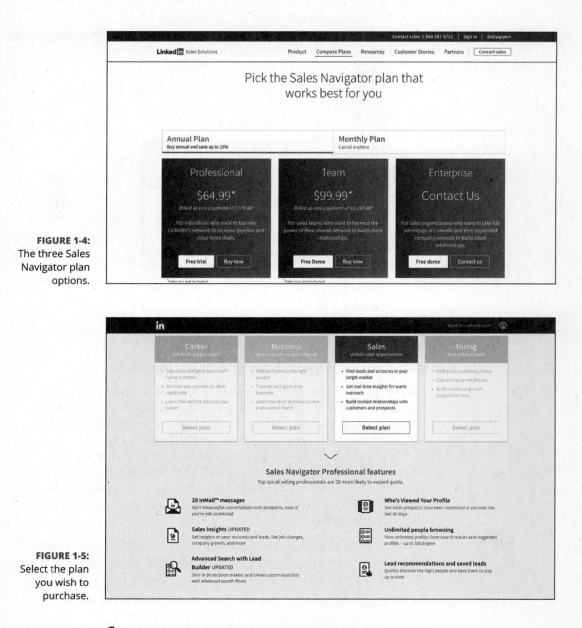

FIGURE 1-4:
The three Sales Navigator plan options.

FIGURE 1-5:
Select the plan you wish to purchase.

6. **Click the Start My Free Month button.**

I know, I know. What do you have to do to actually buy a subscription?! This is a good thing, though! LinkedIn gives you the first month for free, regardless of whether you are ready to purchase a subscription or not. That way, if you decide it's not the right tool for your needs, there's no commitment and you don't lose any money.

7. **Enter your payment information and click the Review Order (for credit card payments) button or the Continue to PayPal button.**

   LinkedIn requires you to either enter in a credit card number or connect your PayPal account to start your trial subscription since you will be charged automatically each month once your free trial month is over. If you click Continue to PayPal, you finish the transaction on the PayPal website.

WARNING

If after you start the free trial you decide you don't want to purchase the plan after all, but you don't cancel within that first month, your official subscription will start and you will be charged.

8. **If everything looks correct, click the Start Your Free Trial button.**

   Congratulations! Now the fun begins!

Measuring Efforts with the Social Selling Index

You're probably eager to jump right in and start tinkering around with your new sales tool. If you take nothing else away from this book, however, take away the fact that you have to have a plan. The saying, "if you fail to plan, you plan to fail," exists for a reason! So, before we get into the nitty-gritty of Sales Navigator, there are a few topics to discuss to ensure you make the most out of your subscription.

The first of those topics is the Social Selling Index (SSI). SSI is the measurement of how your sales activities are performing. Sales Navigator has a special SSI dashboard that paints you a picture of how your social-selling endeavors are going as well as how you stack up against your LinkedIn network as a whole. It tracks your progress over time, showing you where you're performing the best and where there's room for improvement.

As shown in Figure 1-6, the SSI dashboard illustrates how you're performing on each of the four elements of social selling — establishing your brand, finding the right people to connect with, engaging with the data gained through insights, and building relationships with both your sales peers as well as prospects.

FIGURE 1-6:
Get a clear
picture of your
Social Selling
Index on your
dashboard.

The Social Selling Index isn't just some gimmick LinkedIn thought up to give sales professionals something cool to look at. LinkedIn data shows that social-selling leaders — those individuals with high scores in all four categories — create 45 percent more opportunities than their peers with lower scores, and they are 51 percent more likely to reach their sales quota when utilizing this data to improve their social-selling skills. The numbers don't lie, folks! Social selling is imperative for success in sales these days, and keeping an eye on your SSI in LinkedIn is the perfect way to ensure you're staying at the top of your game. Check out Chapter 4 for more details on accessing your SSI dashboard and the importance of always keeping track of your SSI score.

Opening Access with TeamLink

If you have a Team- or Enterprise-level Sales Navigator plan, you have access to an extremely helpful feature called TeamLink. TeamLink is a tool that allows you to view and search the connections of the team members with whom you share a Sales Navigator account.

Even if you're not directly connected to your teammates on LinkedIn (and why not?), you can still view their first-degree connections (in other words, the people they are directly connected to), thereby opening up your network exponentially. You don't have this capability with personal LinkedIn profiles or with the Professional-level Sales Navigator plan.

In the Team- or Enterprise-level plans the TeamLink feature is enabled by default in the Settings menu, which is also where you can choose to turn off the feature if you see fit (but why would you?). With access to this information you can easily see who on your team can connect you with potential leads. The search function even suggests the best path to take in terms of who to leverage in order to make these introductions to the prospect. Everyone knows that one of the hardest parts of sales is having to make cold calls, but with TeamLink, this "call" warms up considerably, increasing your chance of making a successful connection — and maybe even a sale down the line. Sales Navigator even gives you the option to just show TeamLink leads when searching for prospects, as this can often be the most low-hanging fruit.

Planning Your Roadmap for Social-Selling Success

The SSI and TeamLink options are two of the most important (and robust) tools you have at your disposal when you use your Sales Navigator account. Now that you have the ability to identify warm leads (TeamLink), you can focus your social-selling efforts on connecting with those leads all the while ensuring you're on the right track by keeping an eye on your SSI score.

Just like it is with social media marketing in general, utilizing the data generated to improve upon not only how you approach prospects, but also how you interact with them and what information you provide to them, and then adjusting as needed, will really help you move the customer along the sales funnel. Every prospect has his or her own personal buyer's journey. The key to success is being there every step of the way. Let's get started in the next chapter by looking at how to determine your target audience.

Chapter 2

Determining Your Target Audience

I f you don't know who would most likely buy your product, you're not going to be doing a whole lotta selling. You're not going to sell hamburgers and hot dogs to someone who is a vegan, regardless of how gourmet or delicious your food is. While that is a bit of a silly example, it illustrates a point: Don't waste your time on prospects who have no interest in what you are selling. In other words, *know who needs you.* Once you get a handle on your audience, you'll begin to see the importance of personalizing the buyer's journey (which I explain how to do in Chapter 3). Lucky for you, you've come to the right place. LinkedIn Sales Navigator is here to help you narrow down a large audience into a much smaller, highly-targeted audience that represents the group most likely to be interested in your product or service.

In this chapter, I discuss the importance of determining who your customers are through the use of buying personas. I also talk about pain points and how they're the key to connecting with a prospective customer or prospect. Finally, I explain who the other stakeholders are in this buying decision — even though they may not be writing the check — and why it's important to keep these people in mind.

Defining the Buying Personas

Buying personas, also called buyer personas or marketing personas, are detailed profiles of your prospective customers. They go beyond your run-of-the-mill demographic information such as age, gender, and geographical location, however. These personas are given names and occupations. Some sales organizations even use headshots they get from stock photography websites to help their teams get a well-rounded view of the individuals they are looking to target.

Buying personas illustrate the decision-making process of prospects. These write-ups delve into the feelings, concerns, and standards that drive prospects to choose who they're going to do business with, whether that's you or your competitor. This allows sales and marketing teams to tailor two of the three C's of online sales: collecting and connecting. (The third "C" is converting; see Chapter 1 for more information.)

Having buying personas enables sales teams to present the right information (content) at the right time and make a connection at the point in the buying process when that connection is the most likely to be well-received, helpful, and capable of moving the customer to the next steps in his or her buying journey.

Creating buying personas is an important part of the sales process. I'd go so far to say that it is a critical step. When you can visualize prospects as real people instead of just . . . well . . . prospects, it helps you delve into what drives their purchasing decisions.

TIP

Many websites have templates you can download to help you create your buying personas. At the very least, the online versions may give you ideas about what to include in any templates you make yourself. Figure 2-1 offers one example of a buying persona template.

Creating a buying persona is also a good way to begin to develop a list of possible pain points you may encounter when dealing with a customer. (Pain points are discussed in more detail in the following section.) If you know ahead of time the complaints you may encounter, you can start to think about how you're going to approach the conversation. For example, does your company have specific documentation that tackles this issue? That may be a good way to establish yourself and your company as subject-matter experts. While it probably won't be possible to predict every situation you'll encounter, if you have a general idea of how you'd approach common ones, you'll be off to a good start.

While creating actual buying personas is out of the scope of this book, a good resource for more information on collecting such detailed information about your current and prospective customers is *Social Media Marketing All-in-One For Dummies, 4th Edition* by Jan Zimmerman and Deborah Ng.

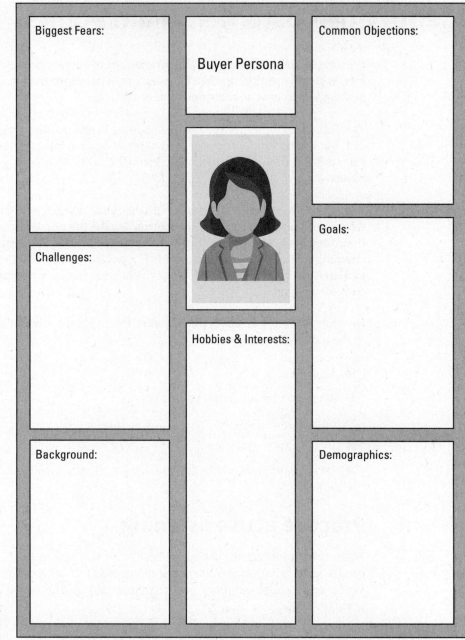

Biggest Fears:

Buyer Persona

Common Objections:

Challenges:

Goals:

Hobbies & Interests:

Background:

Demographics:

FIGURE 2-1:
A sample buying
persona
template.

Identifying Customers' Pain Points

Creating buying personas is an important part of successful social selling, and it assists you in identifying your customer's pain points, or the reasons why they're looking to purchase a product or solution.

Problems need solutions in order to stop being problems. That concept is as old as dirt. But when it comes to sales, there is much more to the equation. In order to be successful in converting customers, you need to know what's going on in their minds.

You already have a general idea about what your customers are looking for. But what is the exact nature of their problem? Maybe the problem goes much deeper than they realize, and they need an entirely different solution. Why are they choosing this solution over another? Is it a certain feature or set of features? Who else are they considering (competitors) and what makes your product and company stand apart?

Here are five ways to identify a customer's pain points, which I explain in detail in the sections that follow:

>> Actively listen.

>> Ask customers about their pain points.

>> Find out what motivates them.

>> Try to find a common ground.

>> Identify what you think the customer's most pressing issue is.

Practice active listening

To meet the prospective customer where he or she is at in the buying cycle, you need to know what got the prospect into the cycle in the first place. You do this by asking open-ended questions and actively listening. The key word in that sentence is *actively.*

Nowadays, our minds are racing at a mile a minute. It's not uncommon for a person to be "listening" and at the same time be thinking about a response even while the other person is still talking. When that happens, there's a greater chance parts of the conversation could be lost. In speaking with a prospect, that could be a devastating setback because you potentially lose information about other pain points or even what the prospect is looking for in a solution.

TIP

Practice active listening. The way we listen now is so ingrained that it's actually fairly challenging to do. But once you get the hang of it, you'll see what a difference it makes and you'll never want to go back to a "lazy" listening style ever again.

Ask customers what their pain points are

This may seem obvious, but prospective customers expect you to ask them this question. After all, you're there to sell them something. But don't lead with pain points as part of the conversation. If you do, you run the risk of falling into the category of being "the typical salesperson" in that you have one goal, and that's to make money off of him or her. Well yeah, you are. But you're there to take care of them as well, and you have to make sure they know that you are there from start to finish. You need to convey that you actually care about helping them. Bury the lead.

Find out what motivates them

If it's a business customer, what is the business all about? What are the company's core values? What drives the company to open the doors every day and continue offering its product or service? When you find out what motivates your customers, you can start to connect the dots about how their pain points fit into — and affect — their business as a whole.

For example, many times the problem goes much deeper than just a content management system (CMS) that isn't meeting their needs. Maybe the CMS isn't meeting their needs because a core value of the company is to always stay ahead of the curve when it comes to providing their customers with top-notch support. But they've been unable to do that because the CMS crashes or perhaps it isn't scalable. Now you know that up-time and scalability is a must-have in whatever solution the customer purchases — two factors he or she may not have come right out and told you.

REMEMBER

You're interviewing and assessing the prospect just as much as the prospect is assessing you. Finding out after the purchase is complete that you can't fulfill the customer's needs because you didn't take the time to find out said needs ahead of time can hurt your business' reputation.

Find common ground

This may not always be possible, but if it is, share a time when you experienced a similar issue or pain point. After all, misery loves company, right?

There's a lot more to it than that, of course. When you're able to empathize with the customer, the customer feels that he or she is truly being heard and that you understand the problem. And what better way to illustrate that you understand the problem then to tell them about a time when you had a similar one and how you overcame the issue? Bonus points if the product or service was what helped fix the problem!

Do not, under any circumstances, be dishonest. Customers aren't stupid, and the chances are good that they will see right through your lies and you and your company will instantly be discredited. It may even go further than that if the customers voice their anger on social media.

Identify the most pressing issue

The customer is looking to you to be the subject-matter expert on his or her pain point. What better way to communicate that then to give your professional opinion about what you think the most pressing problem is and how you suggest it be tackled?

Now here's the hard part: Don't bring your product up at this point in the game. While we all know what happens when we assume, there's a high likelihood that when you give your opinion about the way to solve this issue, the customer will automatically connect the dots themselves when it comes to your suggestions and how your product fits into the equation. It is low pressure and your customer will appreciate it greatly. You'll build up goodwill, which goes a long way when it's time to make the final purchase decision.

Social media is a two-way conversation. It's not the place for overt selling. In fact, if you're constantly trying to push your products on social networks, you'll eventually be seen as a spammer and be ignored, or worse, called out for your activity in a negative way. If people start reporting your nuisance behavior to the social networks, your accounts may even be suspended. Just chill out with the high-pressure tactics.

Who Are the Stakeholders and What Are Their Dreams?

Never forget that there may be many other people affected in some way by the purchase of your product or service. These stakeholders are involved in the buyer's journey, even if they aren't directly involved in the decision-making process.

It's important to keep these individuals in mind when you're going through the process of social selling because the individuals you're dealing directly with will have to answer to these other stakeholders for better or for worse. They are the ones who will be held accountable if the solution they decided to purchase doesn't, in fact, solve the problem at hand and ends up costing the company even more time and money than originally planned.

The decision-makers are going to want to be as educated as possible on all aspects of not only your product, but also where their pain points originated from. Sometimes it's not readily apparent to them, and they're looking for someone to help them sort that out. Sometimes you may encounter a prospect who says, "All I know is that no one is buying our product all of a sudden." You'll have your work cut out for you with that one. But that's what you're there for. You're there to provide them with as much information they need to be able to not only make a purchase decision (hopefully in your favor!), but also be able to justify that decision with the other stakeholders.

So, who could be some possible stakeholders for prospects? Here are a few examples to keep in mind:

>> **Company employees:** This may be an obvious one, but it needs to be mentioned. Sometimes a company's pain point may not directly impact your employees. In the CMS example from earlier in the chapter, maybe the lack of a functioning content management system (CMS) resulted in prospects not receiving the information they were requesting, meaning leads were lost. That lack of revenue very well may mean there are no bonuses for your employees at the end of the year. They definitely have a stake in getting a new system that actually does its job!

>> **The families of employees:** If sales are down considerably, that may mean you have to lay off some of your workforce. Families are going to feel the sting of the loss of income. Lifestyles will change, especially if it ends up being a long-term unemployment situation. An employee's family, while not directly involved in the sales process, will definitely be negatively affected by a purchase.

TIP

Take a look at your own organization. Pretend you had to do without an integral part of your business and think about how far-reaching the effects of that loss are.

>> **Customers:** This may be another obvious one, regardless of whether the company is a business-to-business (B2B) or business-to-consumer (B2C) organization. If the company is having issues with one of its processes or systems, there's a good chance its customers are negatively impacted, and the company will see a drop in sales. If the company's customers can't get what they need, your customer won't be getting what he or she needs.

>> **Vendors:** A drop in sales for a company means budget cuts. Many times, creature comforts are the first to go when a company misses sales numbers and overall revenue starts to suffer. The catering company who handles "taco Tuesdays" for employees may lose a big contract. The printer repair guy may lose a contract because a company will try to fix issues with the printer themselves. This is the trickle-down effect, and it can be far-reaching.

>> **Government entities:** This stakeholder may not have been obvious, but certain government entities may have a stake in a company's purchase. For example, if a company is looking to buy a new online ordering platform that exponentially increases the number of Internet sales it makes, the small-town post office may not be able to handle the increased shipping volume in a timely manner. The staffing changes the post office may need to make in order to keep up with the new orders will mean increased expenses.

Chapter **3**

Mapping the Buyer's Journey

B efore the Internet, customers had to put in a decent amount of effort in an attempt to find solutions to their problems. They had to break out their trusty telephone directories, search alphabetical lists of service providers, and make call after call, all the while hoping they'll come across and ultimately hire the best, most honest person for the job. Furthermore, their options were limited to their general geographical area, so they had even fewer companies from which to choose.

Obviously, that is no longer the case. In fact, I would argue that we, as social-selling professionals, now have to fight "the paradox of choice," the idea that we are so inundated with choices that it causes stress and anxiety and we end up not making any choice at all.

In this chapter, I discuss how to recognize and map the buyer's journey in order to meet your clients where they're most likely to be open to the informational content you have to offer. I talk about how important it is that your LinkedIn profile reflects a customer-centric approach as opposed to an employer-centric one, or worse still, a sales-centric one. Finally, I delve into how to ensure your customers return time and time again — hopefully bringing their friends, family, and colleagues with them.

Understanding Where Customers Do Their Research

The first step along the buyer's journey is when customers realize they have a problem they need to solve. They may not know exactly what that problem is, just that they're feeling some kind of pain point that they want to go away. (See Chapter 2 for more about identifying your customer's pain points.)

This is when customers start their research. If they haven't put a name to their problem yet, they may be researching the root cause of the issue. If they have identified the cause, this is when they start to research different solutions. So, when the time comes when customers are ready to look into how to resolve this pain point, where do they go for information? Well, it probably doesn't surprise you that they go online!

According to the Q3 2017 HubSpot Content Trends Survey, 62 percent of people use search engines to gather information, while 50 percent of the people surveyed said they consult the company's own website. 42 percent head to review websites, and 38 percent ask friends or peers for solution recommendations. In contrast, only 11 percent of people reported getting information from salespeople — the lowest number in all of the categories. If that doesn't tell you the importance of social selling, nothing will!

Why do you think people choose these other (mostly online) methods of research when they're looking for a solution to a problem? There could be a couple of different answers to that question. A big reason is the trust factor. Prospects know that salespeople traditionally have only one thing on the agenda — making the sale by any means necessary. Sometimes this means dishonesty and manipulation, unfortunately. It's because of the unscrupulous behavior of individuals like this that makes it more difficult to gain the trust of consumers today.

When people research the problem and possible solutions online, they can find many different sources of information and then choose which ones to believe and which ones to discard. In other words, they have more control over the information they accept as being the most truthful and helpful. Because there are a variety of sources of information, their confidence is high that they'll be able to locate information to help make an informed decision.

That's where social selling comes into play. Going back to HubSpot's study, 35 percent of people research their options on social media. Since we know that prospects do the majority of their research online, we know where we have to be with helpful and informative content to make the decision-making process as simple as possible.

Meeting the Customer: How Accessible Are You?

When prospective customers are conducting their research, they're not only looking for information regarding potential products or services, they're also looking for companies they feel can meet their needs and solve their problems.

So, how easy is it for them to find you on LinkedIn? Will you turn up right away in their searches for service providers, or will you be at the bottom of the pile? If you happen to make it to the top of the LinkedIn search results, what will they find when they land on your profile? A headline that entices them to click? A list of experiences that have little to nothing to do with what you're actually trying to sell?

TIP

Customers search for specific skills and specialties. Make sure you know the applicable keywords and include them in your LinkedIn profile.

Keep the following questions in mind to craft a LinkedIn profile that not only catches the prospect's attention but also makes the prospect want to click and read more:

>> **Is your profile sales-centric or customer-centric?** Will customers read about how you've been promoted three times in the last five years and have made your company a lot of money, or will they learn that you specialize in helping customers with CMS issues? Or that you have a passion for working closely with your clients from start to finish, ensuring that they're always happy?

>> **Are you offering something of value?** Why should customers click on your profile instead of the one underneath or above yours? What differentiates you from the others who showed up in their search? Do you have some kind of take-away such as a PDF checklist they can download, a cheat sheet, or a video to ensure you stay top-of-mind once they leave LinkedIn?

For example, in my LinkedIn profile, I provide a link to a LinkedIn profile cheat sheet in the Experience section. When people visit the URL to download the cheat sheet and enter their email addresses, they're taken to the page shown in Figure 3-1, where they can click the button to view the cheat sheet. It's a win-win situation because not only do the prospects get some helpful information, but I'm also collecting their email addresses for follow-up.

>> **How easy is it for customers to contact you?** You'd be surprised at the number of profiles I come across where I have to dig deep down into the profile to find contact information — if it's even there. Don't make customers have to work for ways to get in touch with you. Unless you have your own television show on the Home Shopping Network, customers probably aren't going to put in the effort to dig up your contact information.

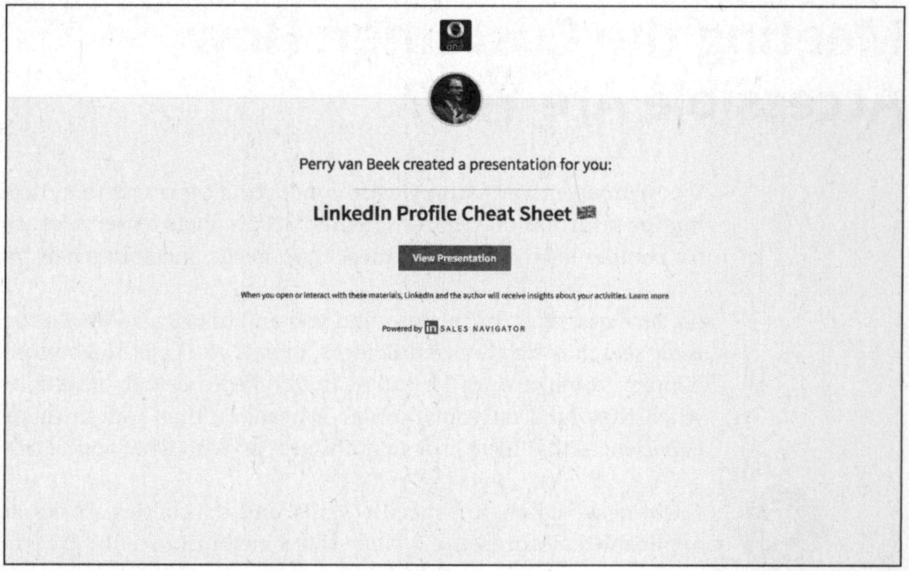

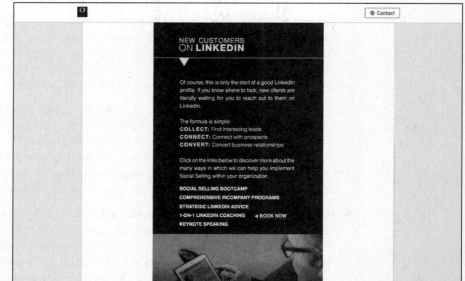

FIGURE 3-1:
Offer a takeaway on your LinkedIn profile to stay top-of-mind when prospects leave LinkedIn.

The same thing goes for any informational material you disseminate. Is your contact information always somewhere on the page? For example, as shown in Figure 3-2, customers can contact me through the Contact button that appears in the top-right corner of the informational page or through my call-to-action link, Book Now.

FIGURE 3-2:
Every page in your informational content should have contact information somewhere on it.

For even more information on how to make sure your LinkedIn profile is the best it can be, I highly recommend you check out *LinkedIn Profile Optimization For Dummies* by Donna Serdula.

Conducting the Transaction: What Motivates Your Customers?

Do you know what motivates your prospective customer? Truly motivates them? In my consulting practice, I regularly encounter salespeople who claim to know exactly what their customers want, but it's usually something that just barely scratches the surface of the problem at hand.

REMEMBER

The customer may want something, but that want is often driven by a need. What is that need? If you can't answer that question, you're not doing a good job of taking a holistic approach to your sales endeavors.

Approaching the sales process *holistically* means you look beyond just the surface problem and the immediate solution that you have to offer. It's about thinking about everything that goes into this pain point. A good way to remind yourself to approach a sale holistically is by making sure you take things back to the beginning and ask yourself:

>> **Who** is affected by this customer's problem? List all stakeholders.

>> **What** is the perceived problem and are there other issues that feed into this problem that may not be considered?

>> **Where** is this problem taking place? Is it in the customer's place of business? Or with the customer's e-commerce site?

>> **When** did this problem start? Had it happened in the past and were other solutions implemented at the time?

>> **Why** is the customer looking into a new solution to his or her pain points now? Did something happen to drive action? Is the customer getting pressure from the senior management at his or her company?

>> **How** does the customer envision a perfect fix to the problem and how does the solution provider fit into this picture?

Creating Fans: Will Your Customers Recommend You?

It's a great honor when customers return to you for assistance when they have problems in the future. It shows that they trust that not only is your product or service of high quality, but also that you, the salesperson, know what you're talking about. You've managed to build up a sense of trust with them.

As wonderful as repeat business is, do you want to know what's even better? When existing customers recommend you to their family, friends, and colleagues. Think about it: They're staking their name and reputation on you and the services you provide. Your existing customers who recommend you have a lot to lose (or at least they're risking a lot of teasing at the water cooler) if you end up being a dud who is unable to help their friends out.

But before you even get to the point where existing customers know and trust you enough to recommend you, you have to rethink the popular saying, "It's not what you know, but who you know." Throw that out the window. Go ahead, I'll wait. All set? Good. Now, here's a short story to show you where your thinking needs to be instead.

Years ago, I met Sir Richard Branson and we spoke briefly. Now I can honestly say that I met Richard Branson . . . pretty cool, huh? But is it really? Would Mr. Branson remember me if I walked up to him on the street or even at a sales conference? As much as I like to think of myself as somewhat memorable, I'm going to have to concede that no, he most likely wouldn't remember me. So, at the end of the day, the fact that I "know" him doesn't help me at all. If I mentioned this story to prospects, do you think this fact would help clinch the deal? Of course not. After all, why would they care?

Back to the "it's not what you know, but who you know" saying we're all familiar with. I challenge you to think of it instead as, "It's not who you know, but who knows *you.*" Taking this a step further, you need to turn your network into fans. *Raving* fans, even. Once you have enough fans, you never have to sell again because your network will be promoting you on an ongoing basis.

REMEMBER

When you're expanding your network, you have to ensure you're building relationships with everyone you add to your network. I'm not saying you have to go so far as to shoot hoops with a few customers every Wednesday and play a round of golf with a few others every Saturday. It means that people won't refer others to you if they don't know you. We call this becoming ATOMIC, or Always Top of Mind In your Community, and it's something every social-selling professional should take seriously.

TIP

More often than not companies are focused on bringing in new clients rather than focusing on retaining their existing clients, yet the likelihood of selling to an existing client is between 60 and 70 percent. In contrast, the likelihood of selling to a new client is only between 5 and 20 percent. It should be apparent where the bulk of your social selling should be focused.

I've talked about how important it is for clients to become fans and recommend you, but how do you ensure people in your customer's network become aware of your relationship and subsequent recommendation? LinkedIn happens to have a great way to showcase all of the recommendations you receive, as shown in Figure 3-3.

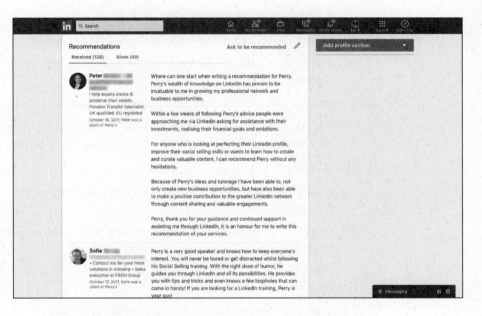

FIGURE 3-3:
The recommendations section on LinkedIn lets your network recommend you to others.

There are two ways in which you can get recommendations on LinkedIn. The first is if the other person takes it upon him- or herself to write a glowing recommendation without you asking for one. The second way is, of course, by asking for one. If you already have a great relationship with the customer and you've given nothing but stellar customer service, chances are good the recipient of your request will be more than happy to accommodate you. Luckily, LinkedIn makes this a painless process.

To ask a contact for a recommendation, follow these steps:

1. **Log into your LinkedIn account.**

The page you land on is the feed that shows all the posts from the people and companies you follow.

2. **Click your name in the box that appears on the left side of the page.**

   It's located underneath your picture and takes you to your profile page.

3. **Once on your profile page, click the Add Profile Section button that appears underneath your profile picture.**

4. **Select Additional Information in the drop-down menu that appears to expand that section.**

5. **Click the plus sign icon next to "Request a Recommendation."**

   A box pops up asking who you want to ask to recommend you, as shown in Figure 3-4.

6. **Start typing in the name of your contact.**

   LinkedIn starts suggesting matching names as you're typing.

7. **Once you find the person you're looking for, click that person's name in the list.**

   Another box pops up asking how you know this person.

8. **Click the drop-down menus that appear to select your relationship as well as the position you were in when you worked together.**

9. **Click the Next button.**

   A box pops up in which you can add a personalized note to the recipient, as shown in Figure 3-5.

10. **Write a short note to your contact, asking if he or she would be willing to write you a recommendation for your profile.**

    You may want to add information about any specific projects you worked on together.

11. **Once you've perfected your note, click the Send button.**

    That's it! Hopefully it's not too long until you hear back from your contact.

TIP

Consider sending the person an email ahead of time asking if it's okay to send a LinkedIn recommendation request. Or better still, call that person, as you'll get much more information from an actual call. Either way, it gives your contact a head's up that a request will be coming in case he or she may have any reservations about writing one.

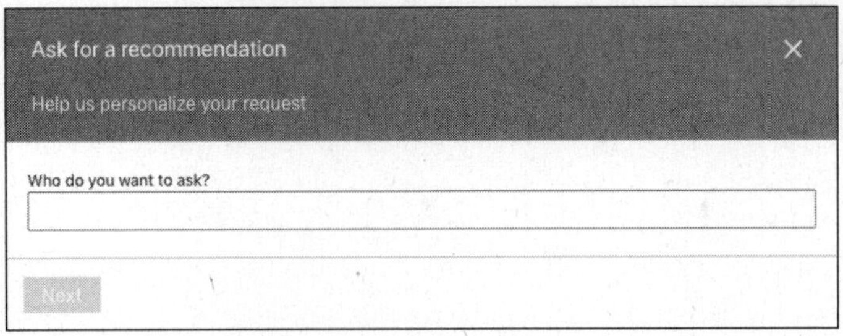

FIGURE 3-4:
Who do you want
to ask for a
recommendation?

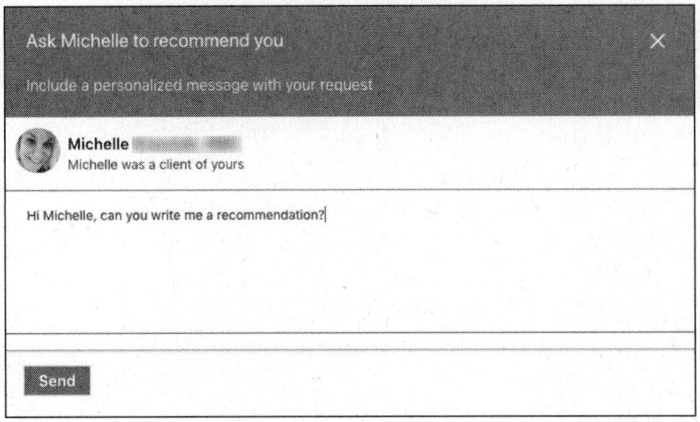

FIGURE 3-5:
Write a
personalized
note.

Up-selling or Cross-selling: Achieving the Customer's Dream

I'll wager a guess that many of you dear readers who saw the heading of this section immediately thought, "Now yer talkin'! Let's talk about the add-ons that really increase our commissions!" Not so fast, cowboy (or girl). Increasing your paychecks should be a pleasant by-product of clinching that up-sell or cross-sell opportunity.

Your goal — what brings the biggest smile to your face — should be that you brought a smile to your customer's face. Whether you landed your customer that promotion, increased the company's sales by 30 percent, or even just made your customers' lives a little bit easier, should be what makes you feel like you've done your job of helping your clients realize their dreams.

Always challenge yourself to see what role you can play in continuously fulfilling the client's dream. Cross-selling and up-selling should always be aligned with the client's dream. Don't just offer products and services without fulling understanding — and being able to explain clearly — how this addition will improve the customer's experience even more.

2

Building a Database of Leads

IN THIS PART . . .

Navigating the important search and filter features of Sales Navigator

Setting your key sales preferences

Measuring and tracking your efforts with the Social Selling Index

Identifying the best leads for your company

Taking advantage of Sales Spotlights to narrow down your search results even more

Saving leads and accounts to refer to at a later time

Chapter **4**

Setting Up for Success

As you probably know by now, LinkedIn Sales Navigator is a robust tool. Much of its power lies just beneath the surface, and the Sales Navigator home page is the gateway to it all. Not only that, but the home page is where you get a quick snapshot of your Sales Navigator world. It's where you see updates from your network as well as get a high-level look at your Social Selling Index (SSI), an important metric to keep an eye on to ensure you're staying at the top of your social-selling game.

In this chapter, I walk you through the different parts of the Sales Navigator home page, explaining what you can do with and access from each section. I give you the low-down on filtering and the importance of being able to find the information most pertinent to you quickly. Finally, I get into the details of such helpful features as being able to view who recently viewed your profile and the fact that your last five viewed accounts and searches are saved automatically.

Navigating the Home Page

There is a lot going on when you first log into your Sales Navigator account and land on the home page. In this section, I give you a brief rundown of the what the different icons and sections of the home page represent. In the following sections, I break down the most important ones into greater detail. Are you ready to roll? Great! (I'm assuming you said yes.)

Main navigation bar

Upon logging into Sales Navigator, you see the home page, like the one shown in Figure 4-1. At the top of the page is the main navigation bar. This is where you switch between the main pages in Sales Navigator. In Figure 4-1, notice that the word *Home* is underlined. This indicates we are currently on the Sales Navigator home page.

When you hover your mouse pointer over one of the other three options in the main navigation bar, drop-down menus appear that give you numerous account-management options. From here you can find updates about your network (Home), saved leads and saved accounts (Lists), both lead and account recommendations courtesy of LinkedIn (Discover), and administrative information about your Sales Navigator account such as usage reporting and seat management (Admin).

On the upper-right side of the home page is an icon that resembles two conversation bubbles. When you hover your mouse over this icon, you get a menu to access your separate Sales Navigator and LinkedIn inboxes. When you have unread InMail messages, a red circle with a number inside it indicates how many new messages are waiting for you. Figure 4-1 shows that I have four unread messages.

Next to the inbox icon is your profile photo. Hovering your mouse pointer over that icon brings up general account settings as well as a few help options in case you get stuck on something. (But that's why you bought this book, right?) You can also access some exhilarating reading in the form of the Sales Navigator user agreement, privacy policy, and cookies policy.

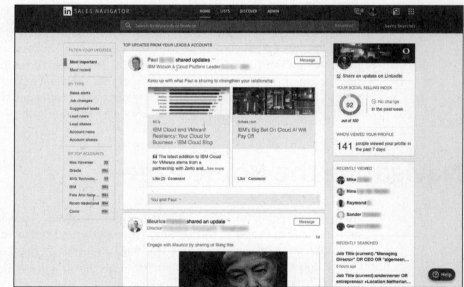

FIGURE 4-1:
The Sales
Navigator
home page.

The icon to the right of your profile photo is for PointDrive, the feature that allows Sales Navigator users with a Team- or Enterprise-level plan to package and deliver content to potential customers. This is a fantastic tool that I discuss in detail in Chapter 7 and tell you how to take advantage of in Chapter 9.

The last icon in the main navigation bar looks like a grid of six squares. It is sometimes called the Work icon and sometimes the More icon. Hovering your mouse pointer over this icon brings up a menu where you can access other LinkedIn-related options, such as LinkedIn Learning, SlideShare, the job posting page, as well as where you can access the Groups that you manage and belong to. (See Chapter 8 for more information about LinkedIn Groups.)

TIP

If you ever want to return to the main LinkedIn social network, it's easily accessible through the grid icon. Because Sales Navigator opens up in a new window or tab when you fire it up from your LinkedIn profile, you can't use your browser's back button to return the main site.

Search bar

Underneath the main navigation bar is the search bar that looks like a typical search bar, but when you click your mouse inside it, it morphs into the super search bar you see in Figure 4-2. Searches are an extremely important part of your Sales Navigator experience, which is why I discuss searching in great detail in Chapter 5.

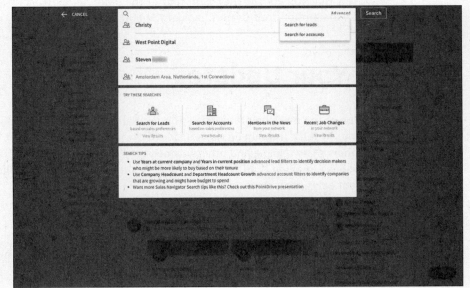

FIGURE 4-2: It's a search bar on steroids.

Update feed

In the center of the home page is the *update feed,* which contains real-time updates about leads (such as when they change jobs), accounts you follow (such as when they make the news), and lead recommendations that are based on your previous account activity like searches. By default, these updates are what Sales Navigator thinks you'd be most interested in seeing.

If you decide you want to switch up the information displayed in your updates feed, on the left side of the page is a box that says, "Filter Your Updates," and you can — yep, you guess it — filter what updates you see in your feed. In the following section, I take you through how to change what is displayed in your feed, in addition to other ways to filter your results.

To the right of your updates feed is a sidebar that is a bit of a catch-all box. It contains a link to post an update to your personal LinkedIn profile and displays your current Social Selling Index score, which I touch on in Chapter 1 but get into more detail about later in this chapter. Underneath your SSI score is a number that shows how many people have viewed your profile in the past week. Clicking that link takes you to a page that gives you even more information about the views, all of which I talk about in a bit.

Last but certainly not least, is the box on the bottom right of the home page that displays both the profile pages and accounts you've recently viewed as well as the things (such as keywords) you've recently searched for.

Now that you got the fifty-cent tour of the place, let's dive a little bit deeper into the most important five sections of the home page.

Filtering Your Updates

One of the most helpful features on the Sales Navigator home page is the "Filter Your Results" section on the left side of the page (see Figure 4-3). Chances are you follow many people and other businesses ("accounts"), so your updates feed will be busy, making it difficult to see updates that are the most applicable to you and your sales goals.

FIGURE 4-3:
The options to
filter your
updates.

Thankfully, you can filter these updates in three main ways to show you only the updates that are the most important to you:

>> **General:** The first two options are Most Important (the default) and Most Recent. When your results are filtered by the Important option, LinkedIn applies some kind of magic (okay, algorithms) to determine what updates it thinks would be of the greatest interest to you based on your site activity. This setting is okay if you're just perusing your feed to get a feel of what's going on in the worlds of those people and accounts you follow. In contrast, the Most Recent setting changes the updates to display chronologically, with the most recent updates placed at the top of your feed. This option is perfect for when you've already caught up with updates and only want to see the most recent ones.

TIP

Always filter your update feed. Sales Navigator is not a social network in the sense of where people hang out and just read update after update from their connections. It's a sales tool and time equals money!

>> **By Type:** This filtering option is more specific than the general option. It lets you filter based on the type of updates, of which there are seven: Sales alerts, Job changes, Suggested leads, Lead news, Lead shares, Account news, and Account shares. Clicking any one of these isolates the updates in your feed that match that particular category. This is helpful for when you want to see

who in your network has recently changed jobs or what kind of content your leads are sharing to their networks.

>> **By Top Accounts:** The final, and more specific, filtering option allows you to isolate only those updates made by the accounts you follow and interact with the most. For example, in Figure 4-3, you see that there are over 99 updates from Oracle and IBM that I need to catch up on. If your sales initiatives are focused on a few specific companies, this filter isolates updates for only those companies you select, making it a lot easier to get caught up on what's been happening in their worlds.

Sharing Updates on LinkedIn

Sharing updates on Sales Navigator is slightly different than posting to other social networks — even LinkedIn. Those sites are designed for people to share information, whereas Sales Navigator is designed more for the consumption of information. That does not mean that one cannot post updates themselves, however.

On the right side of the page is a sidebar that I referred to earlier as a "catch-all box" (refer back to Figure 4-1). At the top of the sidebar right below a miniature version of your profile picture and cover photo is a link that says, "Share an update on LinkedIn." Clicking that link brings up the box shown in Figure 4-4.

In the space where you're to add your update, a helpful reminder says, "Build your presence and brand by sharing content your leads can relate to." If you think your update will hit the mark, type it into the space provided and then indicate whether you want to share the update publicly or just with your connections by clicking the drop-down menu underneath that space. If you want to add an image, click the picture of the camera in the bottom-right corner to locate the file on your computer. Once your update is ready to go, click the Share button.

That's it! Now your update will appear in the feeds of your network connections.

REMEMBER

Your Sales Navigator update feed is not the place to post personal anecdotes or stories!

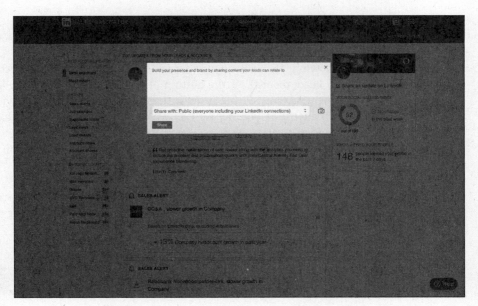

FIGURE 4-4:
Share an update
on Sales
Navigator.

Tracking Your Social Selling Index

I touch upon the Social Selling Index (SSI) in Chapter 1, but let's revisit it since we're in the neighborhood, shall we?

SSI is the measurement of how your sales activities are performing. Underneath the "Share an update on LinkedIn" link mentioned in the previous section is a quick glance at your SSI score. In Figure 4-1, you see that my SSI score is 92. When you click that number, you're taken to a dashboard that paints you a picture of how your social-selling endeavors are going as well as how you stack up against your LinkedIn network as a whole. Sales Navigator tracks your progress over time, showing you where you're performing the best and where there's room for improvement.

In Figure 4-5, you see that my score of 92 out of 100 is made up of individual scores in the four elements of social selling:

» Establish your professional brand

» Find the right people

» Engage with insights

» Build relationships

As shown in Figure 4-6, beneath this graph is another graph that charts how your SSI score has changed over the course of the week (Weekly SSI) as well as a list showing you how you're ranked in comparison to the rest of your team (Team Leaderboard). At the bottom of the SSI dashboard are a few more details about where your SSI fits in with the averages of your team, with people in the same industry as you, as well as with people in your network. This is helpful information to have because if you have a lower-than-average score, you may consider reaching out to some of these individuals for tips on how you could improve your score.

TIP

If your score is higher than average, this may be a great opportunity to mentor more inexperienced social-selling team members. Either way, it's always good to know where you stand in the pack.

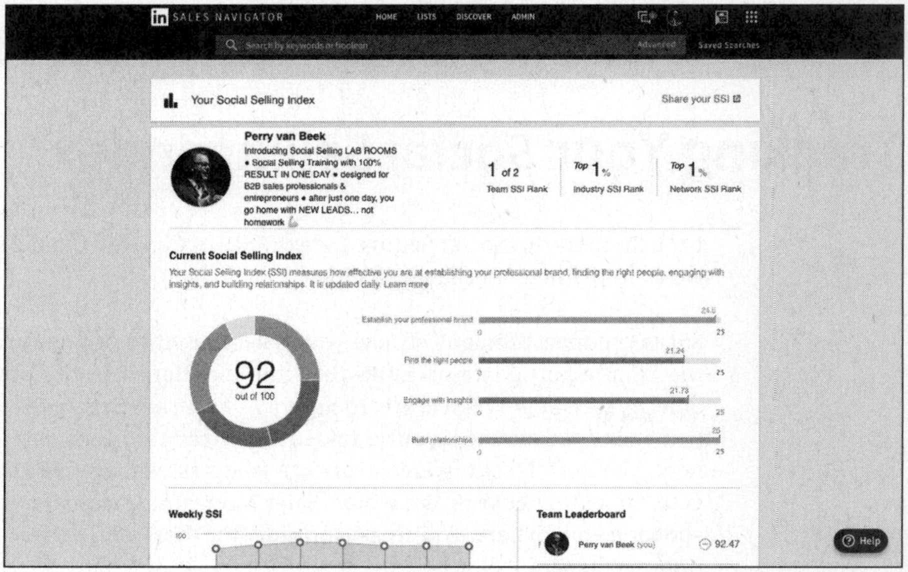

FIGURE 4-5:
The top half of the SSI dashboard shows how you are performing based on the four elements of social selling.

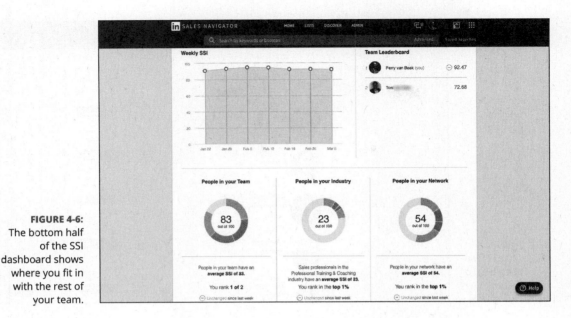

Tracking Who's Viewed Your Profile

What makes LinkedIn unique as a social network is the capability for people to see who has viewed their profiles. When you have a premium LinkedIn account (like Sales Navigator), you can see your profile views for the past 90 days.

REMEMBER

Someone who has set his or her LinkedIn profile to private won't show up in your list of who's viewed your profile. So, despite having a paid account, you won't be able to see whether these people visited you.

In the "catch-all box" on the right side of the home page, you see the heading, "Who's viewed your profile" and a number in large print. In Figure 4-1, this number is 141. That's the number of people who have clicked on my profile in the past week. Clicking that number takes you to the page shown in Figure 4-7 that lists all the people who have viewed your LinkedIn profile. In small print in the top right of this section is the number of people who have visited your profile in the past 90 days. In my case, that number is 2,215.

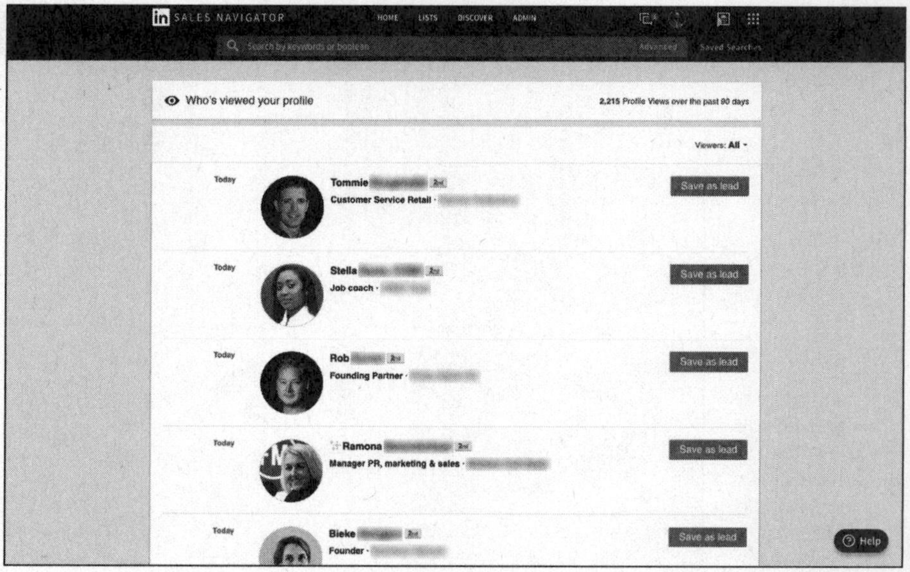

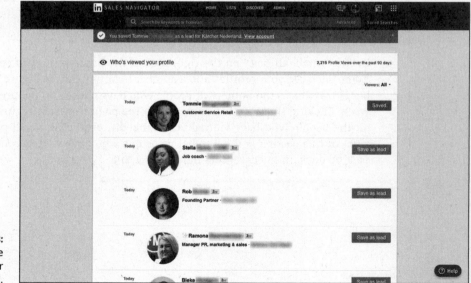

FIGURE 4-7:
All of these people have viewed my profile.

What makes the "Who's viewed your profile" feature different in Sales Navigator is the presence of the Save as Lead button that appears to the right of a person's name in the list. Clicking that button changes it to "Saved," and at the top of the page a message appears that reads, "You saved <Name> as a lead for <Your Company Name>. View account." Figure 4-8 shows you what it looks like when I save one of these entries as a lead.

FIGURE 4-8:
Saving someone who viewed your profile as a lead.

TIP

Clicking the Saved button removes that person from your list of saved leads.

What makes this feature so helpful is the fact that if the person who viewed your profile works at a company you're targeting, you have a soft lead. After all, what made this person check out your profile in the first place? Chances are, he or she came across your name either through a keyword search or because you have connections in common.

Even if the person doesn't work for a company on your radar, it's still good practice to take a closer look at that person's profile and updates to see if he or she is searching for a solution to a problem. In Chapter 2, I talk about the importance of doing your research into a prospect in order to find common ground. The fact that this person viewed your profile is reason enough to start that process.

TIP

When a saved lead looks at your profile, LinkedIn notifies you if you use the LinkedIn Sales Navigator app on your smartphone. (See Chapter 10 for more about the mobile app.) Getting notified that a customer or prospect is looking at your profile is particularly useful information, as it indicates this prospect may be searching for a solution to a problem. This could be a great moment to reach out!

TIP

However, while it's a good idea to regularly visit the profiles of existing customers and prospects, as it may spark a connection or dialogue, you may prefer to check out some profiles without the prospect knowing about it. Good news! There is a workaround to view profiles in private when you wish. You can now differentiate your profile settings between LinkedIn and LinkedIn Sales Navigator. For example, you can select to keep visible only your name and headline in one and set private mode in the other.

Monitoring Your Recent Views and Searches

Last but not least, is the Recently Viewed and Recently Searched sections in the bottom right of the Sales Navigator home page, as shown in Figure 4-9. These sections display the last five accounts you viewed and searches you performed. The searches can be for keywords, individual profiles, or accounts.

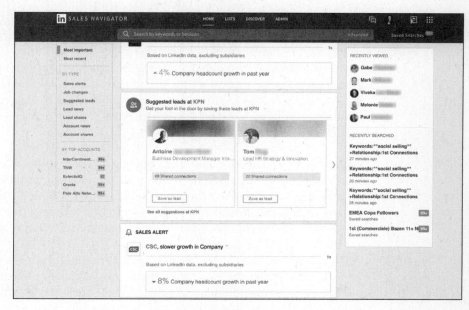

FIGURE 4-9:
The last five
accounts you
viewed and
searches you
performed.

Clicking a name in this box takes you to that person's LinkedIn profile where you can perform actions such as save that person as a lead, send a message, and add tags. (I go into greater detail about identifying leads in Chapter 5.) This feature comes in handy when you start researching a profile or account and then have to move onto something else. Returning to this section makes quick work of picking up where you left off.

The same is true for the Recently Searched section, except it's not only profiles that are kept for easy reference; keywords and account searches are saved here as well, making it easy to refer back to a helpful search you recently performed.

Chapter **5**

Identifying Leads

L eads are the bread and butter of social selling. Heck, it's the bread and butter of *any* selling. It just so happens that finding and collecting leads is what LinkedIn Sales Navigator is all about. (Lucky you!)

Social-selling success is not just about getting leads on paper, however. In order to make the best use of your time and energy, it's important to be able to focus on only those prospects with whom you have the best chance at successfully connecting. There is no use in sending messages to people who haven't been on LinkedIn in six months, for example. To get the most out of your Sales Navigator account, you should master the art of performing successful searches.

In this chapter, I go into the practical details of conducting Sales Navigator searches. I take you through the different types of searches, how to narrow down criteria before the search, and then how to apply the appropriate filters after the search. I also give you a few tips on how to make your searches as successful as possible.

Setting Key Preferences

When first getting the hang of using Sales Navigator, most people stick with general database searches and filter the results as they get them. But as you get to know the program more, you'll learn just how robust Sales Navigator's search functions are, and how much time you're actually wasting by not narrowing down your searches as much as possible right off the bat.

Luckily, LinkedIn makes this easy to do. Simply by setting a few key preferences, you can automatically filter out certain search results, making it much easier to hone in on the leads that are most likely to pan out.

Setting your Sales Navigator preferences is easy. Simply follow these instructions:

1. **From your Sales Navigator home page, hover your mouse pointer over your profile picture in the main navigation menu bar at the top of your screen and select Settings from the drop-down menu.**

   You're taken to the Settings page shown in Figure 5-1.

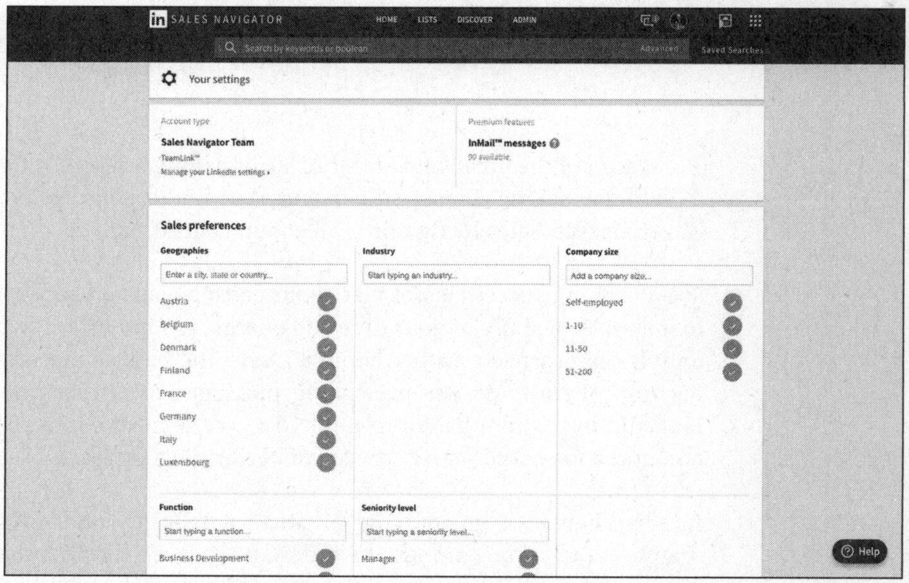

FIGURE 5-1:
This is where you set your sales preferences.

2. **Under the Sales Preferences heading, select the appropriate options by clicking your mouse pointer in the empty text box and typing in your preferences.**

   Sales Navigator auto-suggests matches based on what you type.

3. **Select your preference(s) from the drop-down menu of suggestions.**

   You can select as many as you want without needing to retype your search term.

4. **When you're finished with that section, click Done at the bottom of that section and move to the next.**

If you change your mind about a preference you added, just click the check mark that appears next to the option in the list to deselect it.

Set your Sales Navigator sales preferences as soon as you can in order to save time with your searches.

At the bottom of the Settings page under Sales Preferences are the Email Preferences. Here you can see what Sales Navigator information is available via email and set whether or not you want to receive any. This is important. If you don't manage your Sales Navigator email correctly, you may get, too many messages — leading to the possibility of important ones getting lost in the shuffle. Or you may not enough messages, which may mean you're missing out on some great opportunities.

The default email address where Sales Navigator will send this information is the one associated with your Sales Navigator account. To change that, you have to change the email address Sales Navigator has on file for you.

Figure 5-2 shows the email options available, which include the following:

>> **Account and Lead Updates:** Whenever one of your saved leads or accounts does something such as posts an article or makes a job change, you will receive an email notice about it.

>> **Saved Search Alerts:** If you create and save any personalized searches, whenever something happens that meets the criteria of that search, you will be notified.

>> **PointDrive Notifications:** If you use PointDrive (a presentation management feature included with Team-level and Enterprise-level plans) to disseminate content to your prospects, you will receive an email when there is activity on that content. (PointDrive is discussed in more detail in Chapter 7.)

>> **Who Viewed My Profile Notifications:** When someone views your Sales Navigator or general LinkedIn profile, you will be notified.

>> **Seat Accepted Notifications:** When a team member accepts a seat on your Sales Navigator team, you will receive an email with those details.

Performing a Quick Database Search

The cornerstone of Sales Navigator is its search function, which is broken down into general searches and advanced searches (also called Advanced Search). A *general search*, which we look at in detail in this section, is the search you conduct when you use the search box at the top of the Sales Navigator screen. Don't mistake it for being any less robust or useful than the Advanced Search feature, though! It just has slightly different functionality.

When you click inside the search box at the top of your Sales Navigator home page, you see a drop-down menu like the one shown in Figure 5-3. Note that you don't even have to type something into the search box to get this menu. In fact, if you do type something into the search box, you will get an entirely different result, which I discuss later in this section.

At the top of this drop-down menu are the last five searches you performed using any method in Sales Navigator, regardless of whether you searched for accounts (companies) or leads (people).

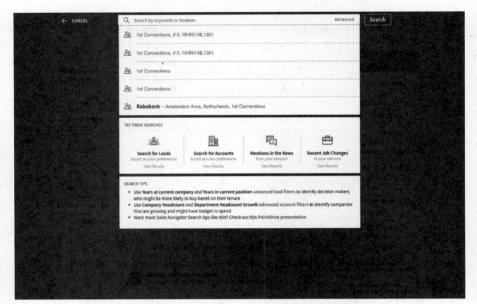

FIGURE 5-3:
The search box
drop-down menu.

Below the searches are additional suggested searches. The additional search options are:

>> **Search for Leads:** This is a search for individuals and is based on your sales preferences (discussed in the preceding section).

>> **Search for Accounts:** This search looks for companies, which is also based on your sales preferences.

>> **Mentions in the News:** Whenever someone in your network is mentioned in the news, you can find it with this search.

>> **Recent Job Changes:** When someone in your network changes jobs, running this search will list them all in one place.

The bottom section in the search box drop-down menu are a few tips from Sales Navigator to make your searches more productive. And to think we haven't even typed a search term into the box yet!

Now it's time to search for a keyword, lead, or account and see the different options Sales Navigator comes up with. In Figure 5-4 you see that I typed in the keyword *social*. The results at the top of the drop-down menu are saved searches I did using that keyword. In the section below, it gives me the option to search specifically for leads that contain the keyword *social* or only accounts that use the word *social* in their profiles. As you can imagine, there are going to be a lot!

Beneath that section in the drop-down menu are matching leads and accounts. This is a quick glance at the top results for a search of the word *social*, in case you're looking for one of the more popular accounts or leads that use that word. If you find what (or who) you're looking for, click the entry to be taken to that particular Sales Navigator page.

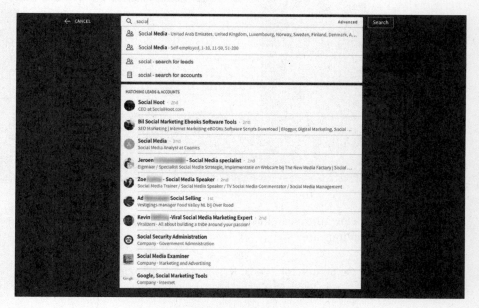

FIGURE 5-4:
Typing anything into the search box results in a drop-down menu of suggestions.

TIP

You can also use a Boolean operator in this search box to narrow your results down even more. Boolean operators are discussed later in this chapter.

Now, on with the search! If you didn't find anything of interest in either of those helpful drop-down menus, click the Search button to the right of the search box or hit the Enter key. At that point, you'll get the long-awaited search results page like the one shown in Figure 5-5.

You'll notice at the top of this results page is a section that LinkedIn calls Sales Spotlights. This section enables you to filter your search results in seven important ways: Total results, Changed jobs in past 90 days, Leads with TeamLink intro (if you have a Team or Enterprise plan), Mentioned in the news in past 30 days, Posted on LinkedIn in past 30 days, Share experiences with you, and Leads that follow your company on LinkedIn (if you have a Team or Enterprise plan). I go through each of these filters and why they're helpful in a later section of this chapter.

TIP

You can add a search result as a lead directly from the search results page by clicking the Save as Lead button that appears to the right of the person's name.

FIGURE 5-5:
The search results page for the keyword *social*.

Searching the LinkedIn Database Using Advanced Search

Whew! If you thought there was a lot of information available with just doing a general search, imagine the kind of data you'll be privy to if you perform an advanced search! The Advanced Search feature has its own page in Sales Navigator, which you access by hovering your mouse pointer over the word *Advanced* in the search box at the top of the Sales Navigator home page and selecting either the Search for Leads or Search for Accounts option.

REMEMBER

You have to choose one of those two options in order to access the Advanced Search page, as there are different search criteria for each option. Figure 5-6 shows the Advanced Search screen for leads.

There are 23 different search criteria you can set on the Advanced Search screen. Yes, 23! I told you this option was pretty darn robust! Here are the different filters available to you when you search for leads:

» Keywords

» Geography

>> Relationship

>> Industry

>> Postal code

>> School

>> First name

>> Last name

>> Profile language

>> Function

>> Title

>> Seniority level

>> Years in current position

>> Years at current company

>> Years of experience

>> Company

>> Company headcount

>> Past company

>> Company type

>> Tag

>> Groups

>> Member Since

>> Posted content keywords

You can narrow down your search results even more by clicking the Show Only TeamLink Connections or Apply Your Sales Preferences radio buttons at the top of the page. When you activate the TeamLink Connections option, whatever filters you apply will only pull up those leads with whom you're connected via TeamLink. (See Chapter 1 for more about TeamLink.) By activating the Sales Preferences option, the filters you set through the Sales Preferences settings are applied before the advanced filters you select here.

TIP

The more filters you apply, the fewer results you'll get. Don't go crazy with your filters because you may end up with nothing!

Using Boolean Operators in Sales Navigator Searches

Boolean operators are words used in searches that instruct the search function to take into consideration the two (or more) words entered in a certain way. The most common words used in Boolean searches are "AND," "OR," and "NOT." Employing keywords when performing searches helps narrow down search results ahead of time, taking away the need for you to go through and strip away any search results that closely match your criteria but are not exact matches.

REMEMBER

LinkedIn requires Boolean operators such as AND, OR, and NOT to be in uppercase.

For example, if you take a look at Figure 5-7, you see that there are over 38 million search results for the term *leadership*. Sales Navigator lists the number of results in the top-right corner of the search screen. Figure 5-8 shows that number increase to just over 43.7 million when the Boolean operator "OR" is added with an additional keyword.

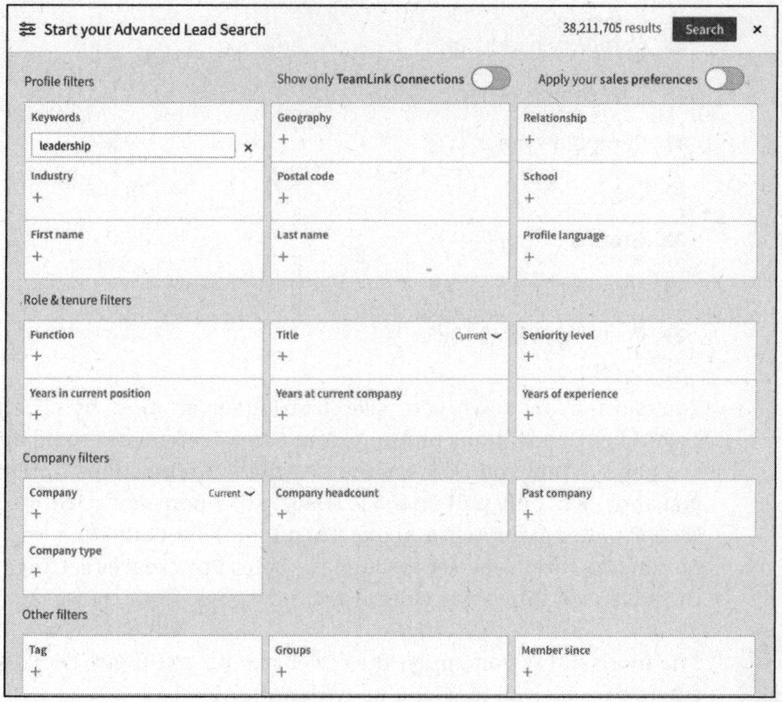

FIGURE 5-7:
A normal search for the term *leadership.*

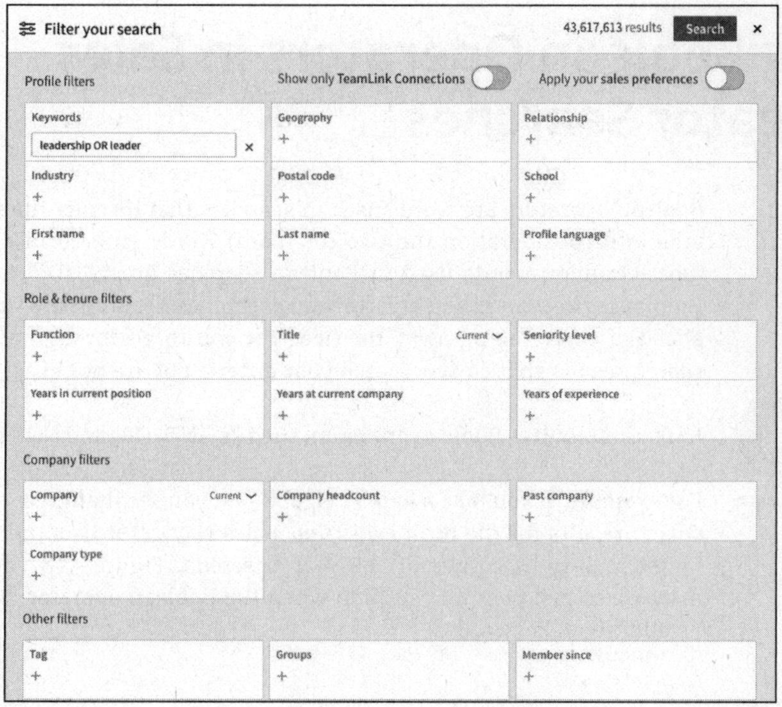

FIGURE 5-8:
A Boolean search for the terms *leadership OR leader.*

Boolean operators are one of my favorite ways to quickly hone in on the most relevant search results. Sure, you can utilize Sales Navigator's helpful filters, but you can get even closer to finding that needle in the Sales Navigator haystack if you perform your search using Boolean operators.

Here are some of the most effective Boolean searches:

>> **Quoted searchs:** When you're searching for an exact phrase (or job title), put those words in quotation marks (" ") and your search results will only return the entries with that exact match.

>> **NOT searches:** Including the word "NOT" (in uppercase) will exclude that specific word or phrase from your search results. For example, if you search for "Junior Project Manager" NOT "Project Manager" the results will not include any people with the title of "Project Manager" and instead only include those people with the title of "Junior Project Manager."

>> **OR searches:** Including the word "OR" in a search returns results that include one or more items in a list. For example, "Harvard OR Yale OR Stanford" will return results that contain any or all of those three search terms.

>> **AND searches:** Typing the word "AND" in a search returns results that contain all of the words you used. For example, typing "Harvard AND Yale AND Stanford" will only return profiles that contain all three of those words.

>> **Parenthetical searches:** When you want to do more complex searches, include parenthesis in your query. For example, if you want to search for "Professors" at Harvard but want to eliminate "Assistant" or "Associate Professors," you'd type "Professor NOT (Assistant OR Associate)."

Customizing Your Search Results

When you have such a robust search function, it helps to have robust customization options to go along with it. After all, there's no use having a large number of search results if it takes you forever to comb through them to find the most relevant ones to pursue.

On the left side of the search results page are a number of ways you can narrow down your search results (see Figure 5-9). They include:

>> **Leads and Accounts tabs:** These tabs display the results for both leads (people) and accounts (companies) that match your search parameters. Your search results are automatically separated, making it even more convenient.

>> **Keywords:** In the Keywords box, you can type in any keywords by which you want to filter your results. You can also use Boolean operators in this search box to narrow your results even more.

TIP

When you first perform an advanced search, all the way at the bottom of the page is the option to search for specific keywords within posted content, not just in profiles or business pages. It's a good idea to make use of this option because you can keep an eye on the keywords your leads and accounts are posting about. If you find they're putting up content that relates to your product or service, it may be a good time to reach out directly.

>> **Exclude saved leads:** This option removes any of your previously saved leads from the search results and is only available on the Leads tab.

>> **Exclude viewed leads:** When you click this option, the search results leads you've already viewed are removed from the list. As with the exclude saved leads option, it's only available on the Leads tab.

>> **Exclude contacted leads:** This filter removes any of the leads you've already contacted from the search results and is only available on the Leads tab.

>> **Search within my accounts:** By selecting this option, only search results from the companies you've saved to your Accounts list are included. It's only available on the Leads tab.

FIGURE 5-9: Filtering your search results helps narrow down the pool of prospects.

There are other (more self-explanatory) filters you can apply to narrow down your Leads search results. These include:

- >> Geography
- >> Relationship (on LinkedIn)
- >> Company
- >> Industry
- >> Company headcount
- >> Function (role)
- >> Title
- >> Seniority level
- >> Tags

TIP

Adding tags to saved accounts and leads helps you quickly locate specific kinds of accounts and leads you've saved. Tags, as well as saving leads, are discussed in greater detail in Chapter 6.

Finally, clicking the View all filters link at the bottom of the filter sidebar takes you to the main Advanced Account Search page shown in Figure 5-10. Just as there are specific filters for Leads, there are also specific filters that apply to the search results under the Accounts tab. These include:

- >> Geography
- >> Industry
- >> Company headcount
- >> Department headcount
- >> Annual revenue
- >> Company headcount growth
- >> Department headcount growth
- >> Fortune (50, 100, and so on)
- >> Technologies used
- >> Relationship (on LinkedIn)
- >> Job opportunities

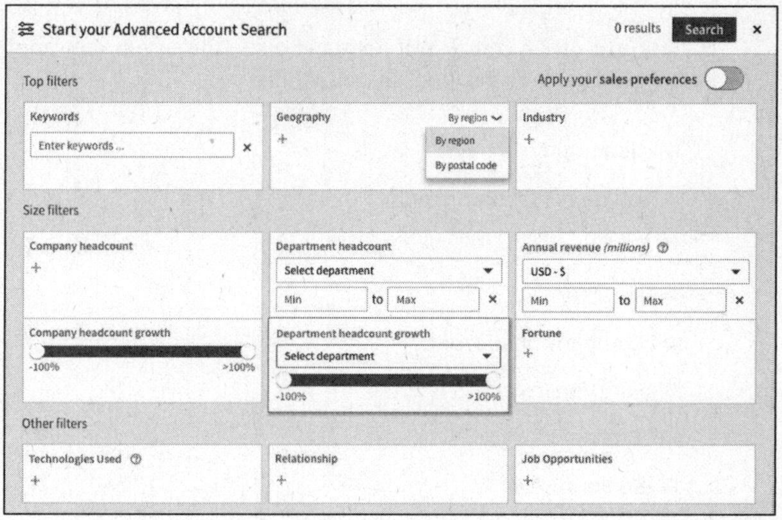

FIGURE 5-10:
The different
filtering options
for the Advanced
Account Search.

> **TIP**
> Clicking the View all filters link at the bottom of the page does not give you any additional filter options.

Saving Your Searches

Saving your searches in Sales Navigator is always a good idea because chances are, you'll be performing that same search more than once. If you're taking full advantage of Sales Navigator's search and filtering criteria, then you'll have developed specific search parameters with which to find the types of leads and accounts you're looking for. It'll save you a lot of time (not to mention headaches) if you save that search so that you can refer back to it (and run it again) in the future.

To save your search, simply click the Save Search link above the Keywords box in the filtering sidebar on any search results page. Once you click that link, you see the Saved Searches screen like the one shown in Figure 5-11. This box not only shows you every search you've saved, but also it shows you how many new results running that search will turn up, the date the search was saved, and whether or not you receive alert email for that search (something I discuss in the next section).

> **REMEMBER**
> You don't want to save every search you perform because then you'll have a long list of them and you may lose track of which ones were the most fruitful for you. In fact, LinkedIn limits the number of searches you can save to 15. It's good practice to focus on the searches you've run in the last year or so.

Saved searches					✕
Name	New Results	Alert	Created		
		Weekly ▼		✓	✕
EMEA Copa Followers Lead Search	184 new	Daily	3/13/2018	✎	🗑
2nd copa followers Lead Search	24 new	Daily	9/22/2017	✎	🗑
Sales Conference Lead Search	11 new	Daily	6/28/2017	✎	🗑
1st (Commerciele) Bazen 11+ NL Lead Search	179 new	Daily	4/13/2017	✎	🗑
CEO etc NL 500+ Lead Search	79 new	Daily	9/19/2016	✎	🗑
Demand Generation EMEA Lead Search	66 new	Daily	9/15/2016	✎	🗑
CCO NL 1000+ Lead Search	133 new	Daily	9/13/2016	✎	🗑
Sales Enabling etc. Europe NOT UK Lead Search	87 new	Daily	7/20/2016	✎	🗑
Sales Enablement OR Effectiveness Lead Search	242 new	Daily	7/20/2016	✎	🗑
CIO / CSO / BDM Amsterdam Lead Search	86 new	Weekly	4/1/2016	✎	🗑
CCO Amsterdam Area Lead Search	134 new	Daily	4/1/2016	✎	🗑
CEO Etc. A'dam 11-200 Lead Search	113 new	Daily	2/11/2016	✎	🗑

((commercieel OR commercial) AND (manager OR director OR directeur)) OR "Managing Director" OR "CEO" OR "algemee

FIGURE 5-11:
The Saved
Searches screen.

Receiving daily, weekly, or monthly email alerts

When you save a search, you're given the option to receive email alerts every time there are new results to check out. The time frames available are daily, weekly, monthly, and never.

I recommend you sign up to receive daily email alerts from the searches that reflect your most active pursuits. In other words, if you're pursuing shipbuilding companies in the Nordic countries at the moment, you'll want to sign up for daily alerts. On the other hand, if you have saved searches from accounts you pursued a year ago, you don't need (or want) daily updates; however, it's always a good idea to keep an eye on things. Monthly is a good option.

REMEMBER

It's important to strike a balance between getting alerts that are immediately useful and getting alerts that are good to have. Everyone's email inboxes are cluttered enough. You don't want to run the risk of not seeing an important alert because it was lost in the shuffle.

Modifying a saved search

Changing a saved search is as easy as clicking a pencil. Icon, that is. To make changes to a saved search, hover your mouse pointer over the Saved Searches link that appears on the right side of your Sales Navigator home page underneath the main navigation menu bar at the top of your screen and click the Edit link at the top of the drop-down menu. You're taken to the Saved Searches screen shown earlier in Figure 5-11.

Once you see the Saved Searches screen, click the pencil icon that appears to the right of the search you want to modify. Once clicked, the search's name and alert frequency become editable, as shown in Figure 5-12. Once you make your edits, click the check mark to save your changes.

TIP

You can delete a search entirely by clicking the trash can icon that appears to the right of the search listing.

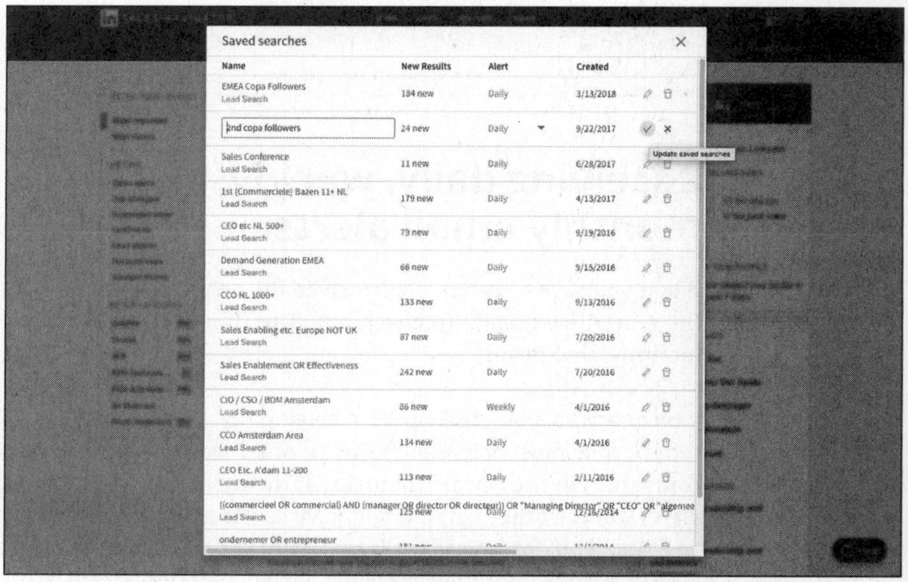

FIGURE 5-12: Here you can edit the search's name and how frequently you get alerts.

Running a saved search again

The whole point of saving a search is to be able to run it again. Sales Navigator makes it easy to access your saved searches. Simply hover your mouse pointer over the Saved Searches link that appears on the right side of your Sales Navigator home page underneath the main navigation menu bar at the top of your screen (see Figure 5-13) and select the search from the drop-down menu that appears. The search opens and you can re-run the search.

If you do not see the specific search you are looking for in the drop-down menu, select the View All link at the bottom of the menu and you'll be taken to the same Saved Searches screen shown in Figure 5-11.

FIGURE 5-13:
Use this drop-down menu to rerun saved searches.

Zeroing in on the Best Results with Sales Spotlights

Sales Spotlights is a LinkedIn feature that uses LinkedIn's data to pick out the prospects in your search who are most likely to be receptive to your communications. Sales Spotlights are located above your search results and are only available on the search results page. Clicking within each section highlights it, indicating that the results you see reflect that specific Sales Spotlight.

The first section in the list is the search's Total Results. It's exactly what it sounds like: all your search results, without being segmented down into the specific Sales Spotlights. Total Results always shows the highest number of results and is the default view on your search results page (see Figure 5-14).

REMEMBER

Keep in mind that the more criteria you enter before the search and the filters you apply after the fact can greatly reduce your total results.

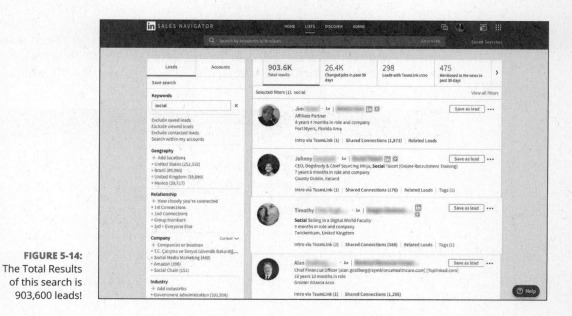

FIGURE 5-14:
The Total Results
of this search is
903,600 leads!

The Sales Spotlights that follow Total Results are broken down into these six categories:

>> Changed jobs in past 90 days

>> Leads with TeamLink intro

>> Mentioned in the news in past 30 days

>> Posted on LinkedIn in past 30 days

>> Share experiences with you

>> Leads that follow your company on LinkedIn

I describe each in the sections that follow.

Changed jobs

The Sales Spotlight to the right of Total Results is "Changed jobs in the past 90 days," which displays the number of leads in this search results list that have recently made a career change in the past 90 days, whether that is changing companies, taking a new position at the same company, retiring, or becoming unemployed. This change is displayed with the words *New role* in blue underneath the person's profile blurb. It also lists the lead's new job, company, and how long the person has been in this new position.

Knowing that someone has changed jobs is helpful for a few reasons. First is the fact that this change may have made this lead a closer connection to you, whether it's through your general LinkedIn network or your colleagues through TeamLink. It just may mean a warmer introduction for you.

The second reason this information can be helpful is if you're already familiar with the company or even the person who previously held that position. It's a great "in" when reaching out to introduce yourself.

The final reason why this is good information to have is because it simply gives you a reason to reach out. It's common for people on LinkedIn to congratulate others on new positions. While you may not know the lead personally, that is a legitimate reason for reaching out. Figure 5-15 shows the search results of those leads who have recently changed jobs.

FIGURE 5-15: The words *New role* appear underneath the person's profile blurb when he or she has changed jobs.

TeamLink leads

The Sales Spotlight section, "Leads with TeamLink intro," indicate how many search results are connected to you via your own team. These TeamLink leads are unique in that you have built-in warm introductions to prospects because they are already connected to your team members.

REMEMBER

Only those with a Team-level plan or an Enterprise-level plan have the TeamLink feature.

To call out an available TeamLink connection, Sales Navigator includes a link with the words *Intro via TeamLink* followed by a number in parenthesis. This number represents the team members who are connected to that individual and able to give you a warm introduction. To see who those team members are, click that link, at which point those team members' profile blurbs appear underneath the lead entry (see Figure 5-16). I discuss TeamLink in more detail in Chapters 1 and 12.

TIP

I cannot stress enough the importance of utilizing your TeamLink connections! It opens up your network exponentially and is essentially a foot in the door to leads you otherwise wouldn't have access to.

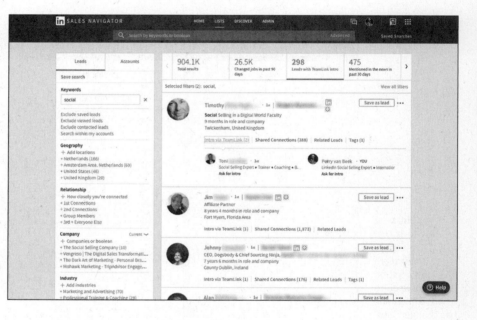

FIGURE 5-16:
You can easily see which search results you can connect with more easily via TeamLink.

Mentioned in the news

Another great way to break the ice with someone is by mentioning something they've done that was published in the news media. This is the purpose of the Sales Spotlight section aptly titled "Mentioned in the news in past 30 days."

These search results will contain some of the biggest names in the industry or industries you're searching in. For example, in Figure 5-17 you can see that the search results for the word *social* resulted in the top two profiles in the list being from some of the most well-recognized (and respected) names in the social media world.

This is a perfect reason to reach out to a prospect. After all, who doesn't like to be written up in the news (for a positive reason, at least) and for your professional network to have seen it? Tell the prospect you saw the piece and add in an anecdote or two related to the subject matter to let that person know that you paid attention and actually care.

TIP

Do actually read the article and check to see if it's the correct person. For example, there are 13 John Jones who work at IBM. Did LinkedIn pick up on the correct John Jones? Plus, actually reading the article gives you a greater chance of engaging with that person with actual insights.

REMEMBER

LinkedIn doesn't monitor every news outlet in the world, so just because you don't see a mention in your feed, doesn't mean the company isn't making the news! It's a good idea to supplement this filter with a general search on your favorite search engine.

FIGURE 5-17:
See which of your connections was recently published in the news.

Posted on LinkedIn within the past 30 days

There's nothing worse than putting blood, sweat, and tears into social selling on LinkedIn and not get any bites because people just aren't on their LinkedIn accounts that often. That's where the "Posted on LinkedIn in past 30 days" Sales Spotlight filter comes into play (see Figure 5-18).

Gone are the days of sending out InMails or messages to people who aren't active on the site only to have them languish, unread, in inboxes everywhere. Not to mention the fact that you may actually be wasting your limited number of monthly InMails and have nothing to show for it. With this filter, now you can see who has logged into his or her LinkedIn account in the past 30 days, making it easy for you to decide whether or not you want to take the chance on a prospect who may not be an active user of the social network.

FIGURE 5-18:
These individuals
are active on
LinkedIn.

Shared experiences

In Chapter 8, I talk about different ways to connect with leads, and the Shared Experiences results screen is the perfect place to start collecting those ideas. As you can see in Figure 5-19, the "Share experiences with you" Sales Spotlight notes when you have things in common with a lead, such as the LinkedIn Groups you both belong to.

Being able to approach a lead with a shared experience makes you seem less like a stranger. Sure, you may start the conversation based on the commonalities Sales Navigator pointed out, but chances are, once you start communicating with the person, there will be more. People buy from people they know, like, and trust. Leverage these shared experiences to get your foot in the door.

FIGURE 5-19: These people share experiences with me.

Leads that follow your company page

If you took the time to check out the lead's profile, then obviously that person is on your radar. For Sales Navigator users with a Team-level or Enterprise-level account, the final section in the Sales Spotlight, "Leads that follow your company on LinkedIn," shows the leads that follow your company page (see Figure 5-20). That means that you and/or your company are on the radar of the leads in these results. How's that for a foot in the door?

How can you leverage this information? If they're aware of your company, chances are they're more open to a "cold call" than someone who isn't aware of it. Knowing that the lead is already aware of your company is a great sign, and it's one you should take advantage of!

FIGURE 5-20:
These leads are
interested in
what your
company is up to.

PRO TIP: SHARING YOUR SEARCH RESULTS

It's never a good idea to act like you're an island when you're a part of a sales team. There may come a time in the future when you could use the help of your coworkers, so why not lend them a hand if you see an opportunity to do so? If you come across any search results you think would be of interest to them, pass them along! Simply copy and paste the url from your browser and send it to them. You'll be glad you did when they return the favor in the future.

Chapter **6**

Saving Leads and Accounts

LinkedIn Sales Navigator wouldn't be, well, Sales Navigator, if it weren't for leads and company accounts. While the robust search functionality is helpful in locating potential leads, being able to save leads and accounts to have quick and easy access to them in the future streamlines your sales workflow.

In this chapter, I show you different ways to save leads as well as where to look to get more lead recommendations. I also take you through how to add tags and notes to both your leads and company accounts. Finally, I show you how you can view and add similar companies suggested by LinkedIn, giving you the opportunity to grow your sales account list without much effort.

Saving a Lead

In Chapter 5, I detail how to identify leads using database searches and the Advanced Search feature (among other ways). If that was the meat and potatoes of Sales Navigator, then this chapter is the gravy and butter you used to enhance your meal. (Sorry, it's lunchtime.)

There will be times when you won't have the ability to immediately follow up on leads, so being able to save them to return to later is crucial. Luckily, Sales Navigator provides you ways to save leads every step of the way. The two main ways you can save leads with Sales Navigator are from a company's LinkedIn page and from a search results page.

From a company's account page

To save a lead directly from a company's business account page, follow these steps:

1. **Type the company's name into the search box at the top of your Sales Navigator home page and select the appropriate company from the drop-down menu that appears.**

You are taken directly to the company's account page, as shown in Figure 6-1.

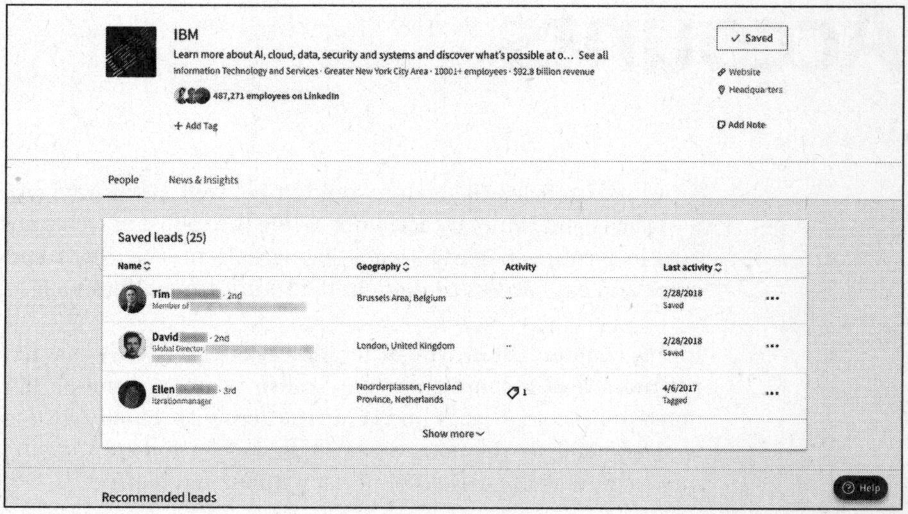

FIGURE 6-1: The company account page for IBM.

2. **From the People tab (the default view), scroll down to the Recommended Leads section.**

If you've already saved leads from the company, Recommended Leads appears after the Saved Leads section you see in Figure 6-1. If this is your first saved lead at this particular company, you won't have a Saved Leads section.

3. **Find the name of the person you want to save as a lead and click the Save link at the bottom of that person's contact card, as shown in Figure 6-2.**

The Save link changes to "Saved" with a check mark next to it. This person is now saved in your leads list.

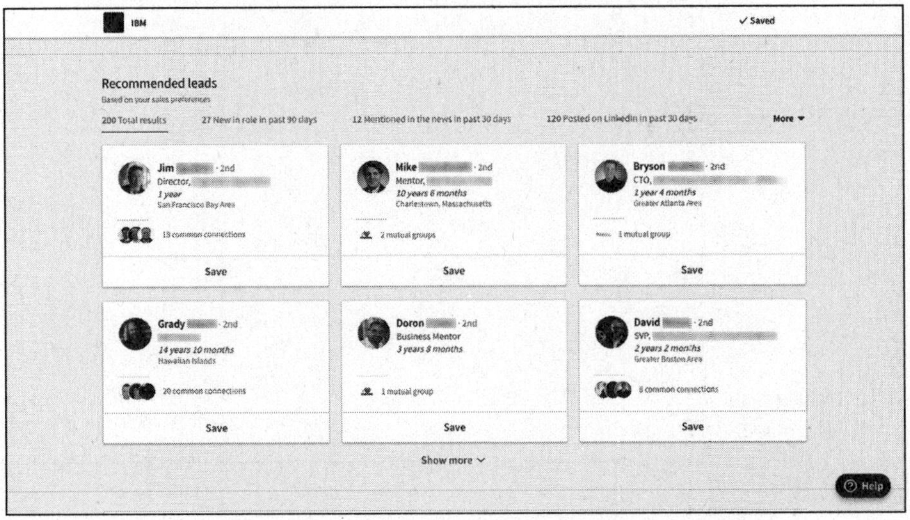

FIGURE 6-2:
Clicking Save adds the prospect to your leads list.

From a search results page

To save a lead from a search results page, follow these steps:

1. **On your Sales Navigator home page, hover your mouse pointer over the Advanced link to the right of the search box at the top of the page.**

Select "Search for leads" from the drop-down menu that appears to open the search criteria box as shown in Figure 6-3.

2. **Enter your search criteria.**

The more criteria you enter, the fewer — but more targeted — results you get. You can see how your lead pool is affected by selecting different criteria by keeping an eye on the number to the left of the Search button at the top of the search criteria box.

3. **Click the Search button that appears in the top right of the search criteria box.**

A results page like the one shown in Figure 6-4 appears.

4. **Click the Save as Lead button to the right of any of the search results.**

The person's profile is saved and a Message button appears in place of the Save as Lead button.

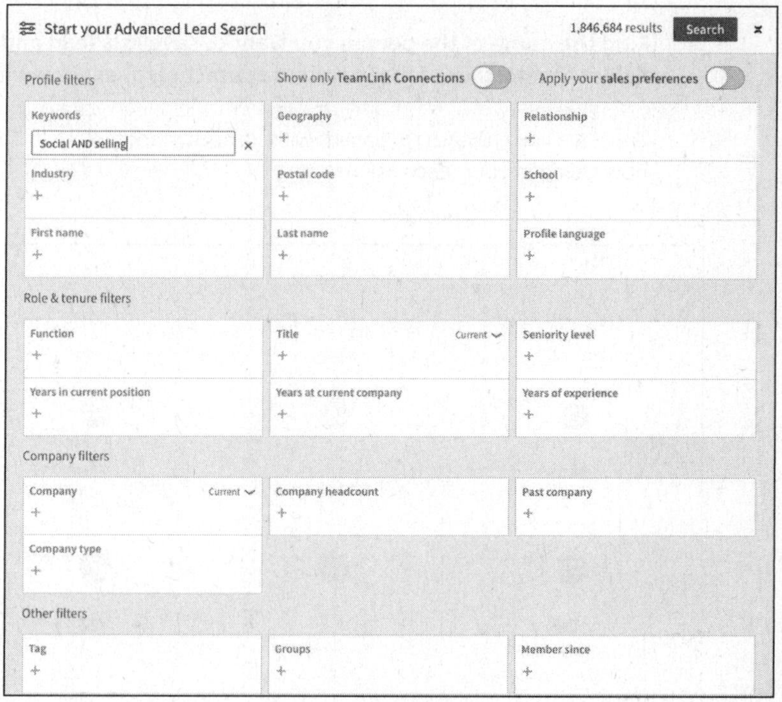

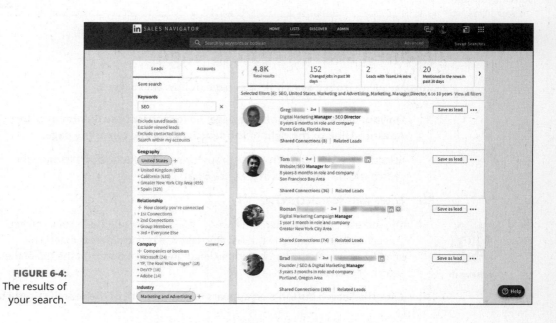

FIGURE 6-3:
So many search options!

FIGURE 6-4:
The results of your search.

TIP

If you accidently mark someone as a lead and want to deselect that person, hover your mouse pointer over the icon that looks like three dots to the right of the Message button and select Remove Lead from the drop-down menu.

Adding Tags and Notes to Your Leads

Sales Navigator has two helpful features to keep your leads organized: tags and notes. *Tags* group leads together in ways that make the most sense for your organization and sales goals. Tags help you streamline your workflow so you can find what you need fast. *Notes,* on the other hand, is a way to store information about leads, such as the last time you touched base with them or the types of content they respond best to, just like you would on a paper notepad.

Adding tags to your leads and accounts is extremely important. After all, the Sales Navigator search function is so robust that you will quickly build up your network (as well as leads and accounts lists). To keep everything organized and easily accessible, you should add tags to be able to locate specific people and companies as quickly as possible.

So, what kind of tags should you use? The answer depends on your industry and company. For example, does your company's industry have some niche areas that you want to keep separate? Why not add tags to identify those particular areas? You can then keep track of leads and accounts that meet that criteria.

In addition, chances are your company uses certain terminology to identify prospects. Maybe this terminology is unique to your company, or maybe it's common terminology. Whatever the case, add these terms as tags to applicable prospects in order to narrow them down in your search results when the time comes.

Another method I find helpful is to tag prospects with the roles they play in their companies' decision-making process. For example, someone might be the final decision maker, an influencer, and so on. That way, you know what kind of content — and contact — is most appropriate when interacting with this lead.

You can also tag leads and accounts based on where they are in the buyer's journey. (For more on the buyer's journey, check out Chapter 3.) For example, are they still in the research phase? Tag them as such so you know how to follow up and what kind of content may be of interest to them.

In Chapter 8, I discuss the importance of building a rapport with prospects. After all, wouldn't you prefer to make a purchase from someone who took the time to get to know you enough to determine that you have things in common? It's the same with leads, which is why it's helpful to add tags that remind you of any commonalities you may have. For example, are you both fans of the New York Yankees? Add that as a tag. How about the fact that you both vacation at Disney World once a year? Tag that lead's account with that. It'll give you something to refer back to when the time comes to reach out in the future.

Now, here's where you put the rubber to the road and start adding those tags. You can add tags and notes to your leads in two ways: from a lead's profile page and from a search results page. Here's how to do it from a lead's profile page:

1. **Go to the person's profile page in Sales Navigator and click the +Add Tag link that appears in the right sidebar, as shown in Figure 6-5.**

   If you've created tags before, they appear in a drop-down menu with check boxes next to them. If you have not created any tags before, Sales Navigator provides a list of six tags to get you started: Customer, Decision Maker, Follow Up, High Priority, Influencer, and Opportunity. There is also a Create New link at the bottom of the menu to add your own tag.

   Sales Navigator provides a list of tags to get you started, but I recommend you start adding your own right away.

2. **Select all the applicable tags (or create new ones) and click the Apply button at the bottom of the box.**

   The tagging box disappears and you're back on the lead's profile page.

3. **If you decide you want to edit or delete tags from your existing list, click the +Add Tag link and select the Edit Tag List link at the bottom of the drop-down menu.**

   In the box that appears, you can either edit what the tag says by clicking the pencil icon next to the tag or delete it entirely by clicking the garbage can icon.

To add a note to a lead's page, simply click the Notes tab next to the Tags tab in the right sidebar of a person's profile page and start typing! (See Figure 6-6.)

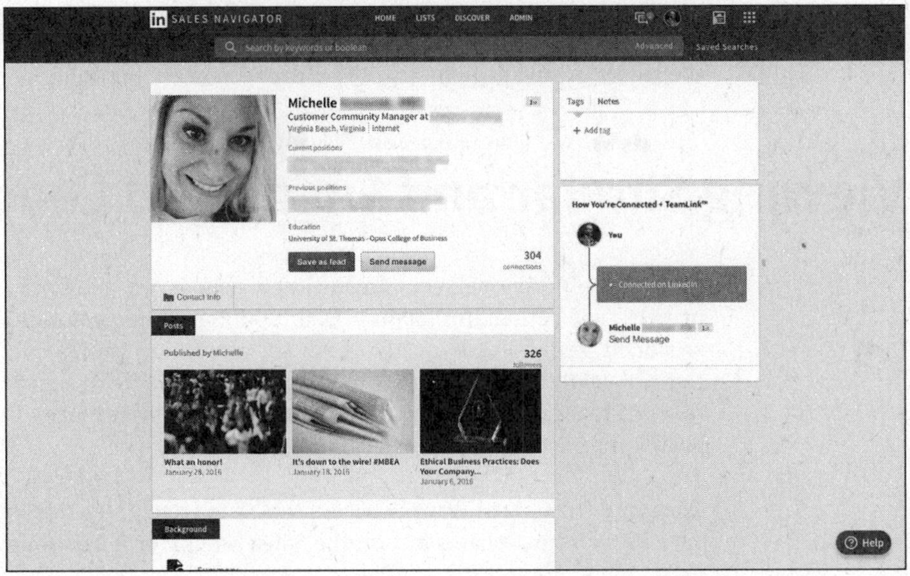

FIGURE 6-5:
Click the +Add
Tag link to add a
custom tag.

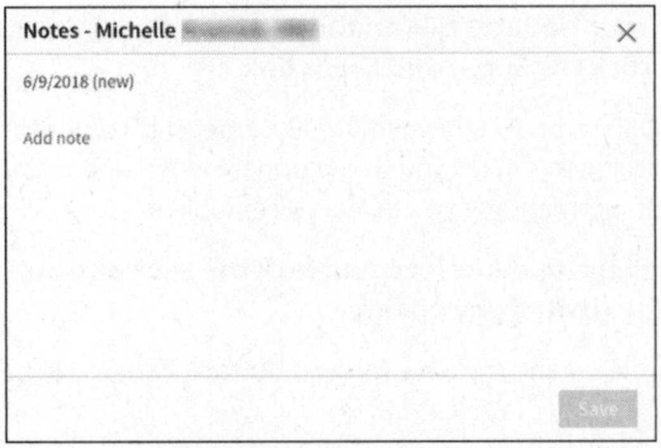

FIGURE 6-6:
Adding a note to
a lead's page.

To add tags to a lead from the search results page, follow these steps:

1. **Perform a search in Sales Navigator.**

You can search via the main search box at the top of the page or run an advanced search.

2. **Once you locate the lead in the search results page, hover your mouse pointer over the icon that looks like three dots and select Tag from the drop-down menu that appears.**

You're presented with the same menu you see when adding tags from a person's profile page, as is discussed in the preceding section. Simply follow Steps 2 and 3 to add tags to this lead.

WARNING

You cannot add a note to a lead via the search results method. You have to be on the lead's profile page in order to utilize the notes function.

Viewing Similar and Suggested Leads

As a sales professional, you already know your target audience. You know the title or titles you're looking for in a lead. You know the geographical area. But even seasoned professionals need a fresh set of eyes on things every now and again, right? Luckily for us, Sales Navigator offers us a fresh perspective by applying more of its searching magic in the form of sales preferences, search history, and profile interaction data to offer us suggested leads.

There are a couple of ways to access this data from Sales Navigator. The first is in your Filter Your Updates box on the Sales Navigator home page:

1. Go to your Sales Navigator home page.

2. In the Filter Your Updates box on the left side of your Sales Navigator home page, click the Suggested Leads link.

This link is the third option down in the "By Type" category, as shown in Figure 6-7. Clicking this takes you to the updates feed of the leads Sales Navigator is recommending you take a closer look at.

3. Scroll through the updates feed and click the Save as Lead button that appears to the right of any update.

The box disappears and the Save as Lead button changes to "Lead Saved."

TIP

If you decide you don't want to save the lead after all, just click the Lead Saved button again to deselect the lead.

The second way to view similar leads is from the main navigation menu bar at the top of the Sales Navigator home page:

1. From your Sales Navigator home page, hover your mouse pointer over the Discover link in the main navigation menu bar at the top of your screen and select Recommended Leads from the drop-down menu that appears.

You are taken to the screen shown in Figure 6-8. These results are based on the sales preferences you set as well as your previous account activity.

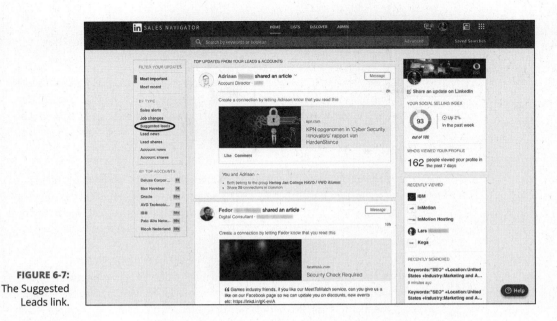

FIGURE 6-7:
The Suggested
Leads link.

2. **Use the filtering criteria on the left side to narrow down your options.**

Chances are, not every lead presented is going to be applicable. Save time and frustration by using the numerous criteria presented to include only those leads that are the best fit for your sales goals.

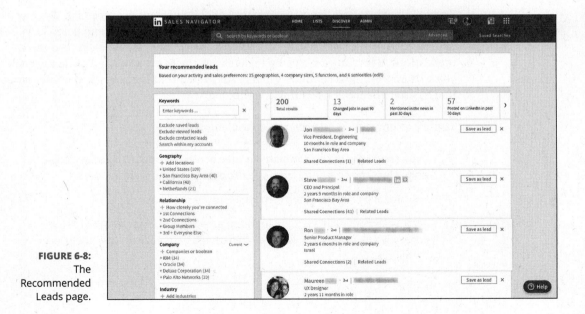

FIGURE 6-8:
The
Recommended
Leads page.

Saving an Account

Saving individual leads isn't the only way to build up your prospect list. When you save a company as an account, you begin to see the company's updates in your news feed as well as additional insights from Sales Navigator such as lead recommendations. Being able to keep up to date with the latest news at a company gives you a chance to find a common ground. And when that happens, a cold lead has a much better chance at becoming a warm one.

To save a company as an account, do the following:

1. **Type the name of the company in the search bar at the top of the page and select the company from the drop-down menu that appears.**

   You are taken directly to the company's business account page.

REMEMBER

   If you've already saved a company as an account, you won't be taken to the company's page. Instead, you are taken to a page that shows the employees of that company.

2. **Click the Save button that appears at the top right of the company's profile page.**

   The company is now saved to your Accounts list. From now on, whenever you search for this particular company, you will be offered a lot more information to select from in the drop-down menu, as shown in Figure 6-9.

   To unsave a company, click that same Save button (which now says "Saved" preceded by a check mark). When the company is unsaved, a green notification box appears on the bottom-left side of your screen.

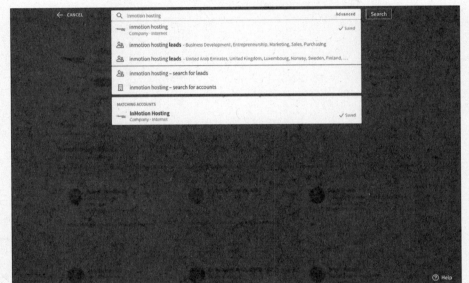

FIGURE 6-9:
Access a lot more information about a saved company account when performing searches.

REMEMBER

When you want to access your saved leads and accounts in the future, simply hover your mouse pointer over the Lists link in the main navigation menu bar at the top of your screen and select one of the two from the drop-down menu.

Adding Tags and Notes to Your Accounts

Adding tags to your company accounts serves the same purpose as adding tags to individual leads. Tags help you keep your accounts organized by whatever criteria you choose, making it easier to find what you're looking for. For example, if in the future you'll want to quickly identify all companies that specialize in a certain product or service, you'd tag those companies with that descriptor and be able to narrow down search results using that word or words.

To add tags to accounts, follow these steps:

1. **Hover your mouse pointer over the List link at the top of the page and select Saved Accounts from the drop-down menu that appears.**

You're taken to the Your Saved Accounts page, as shown in Figure 6-10.

2. **Search for a specific company by typing its name in the Keywords box on the left side of the screen.**

The company you're looking for will show up on the results page. If there are multiple companies with similar names, you may have to scroll down a bit to locate the exact one.

3. **Click the company name to be taken to that company's account page.**

On the company's account page, you see information such as the company description and website as well as any saved leads you may have that are associated with that company.

4. **Click the +Add Tag link that appears underneath the company name and description at the top of the page.**

As with individual tags, if you've created tags before, they appear in a drop-down menu with check boxes next to them. If you have not created any tags before, you only see the six tags Sales Navigator provides. There is also a Create New link at the bottom of the menu.

5. **Select all applicable tags (or create new ones) and then click the Apply button at the bottom of the box.**

If you select existing tags and also add new tags to the list, after you click the Apply button, click the +Add Tag link again and this time, click the Create New link at the bottom of the drop-down menu.

6. **If you decide you want to edit or delete tags from your existing list, click the +Add Tag link and select the Edit Tag List link at the bottom of the drop-down menu.**

In the box that appears you can either edit what the tag says by clicking the pencil icon next to the tag or delete it entirely by clicking the garbage can icon.

TIP

To add a note, simply click the Add Note link on the top right of the company's account page and start typing the note in the pop-up box that appears.

Viewing Similar and Suggested Accounts

When you first join Sales Navigator, LinkedIn presents you with a number of relevant accounts that you may already be selling to in order to build up your initial list. Sales Navigator determines which accounts to show you based on your recent actions on LinkedIn, such as your profile views, company page views, InMail activity, and more.

To add one of the accounts recommended by LinkedIn, do the following:

1. **Click the Save Account button that appears below the name of the account you'd like to save.**

You can add as many of the suggested accounts as you'd like.

2. **Click the Continue button.**

The accounts you selected are now accessible via the Accounts page.

Alternatively, you can hover your mouse pointer over the Discover link in the top menu bar and select Suggested Accounts from the drop-down menu.

Once you have built up a number of saved accounts, Sales Navigator is able to collect your usage data and start to show you similar companies that may be of interest to you. To see these saved companies, follow these steps:

1. **Hover your mouse pointer over the Lists link at the top of the page and select Saved Accounts from the drop-down menu that appears.**

   You're taken to your Saved Accounts page (refer to Figure 6-10).

2. **Locate a company that fits the criteria of other companies you're looking for.**

   For example, if you want Sales Navigator to suggest housewares importing companies, locate a company of that type in your Saved Accounts list.

3. **Once you locate a company, hover your mouse pointer over the icon that looks like three dots that appears to the right of the company name.**

   A drop-down menu appears, as shown in Figure 6-11.

4. **Select the View Similar option.**

   The screen refreshes with a new list of companies that are similar to the one you already have saved.

5. **Click the Save as Account button next to the name of any company that fits your criteria.**

   That's it! You've now added even more companies to your list.

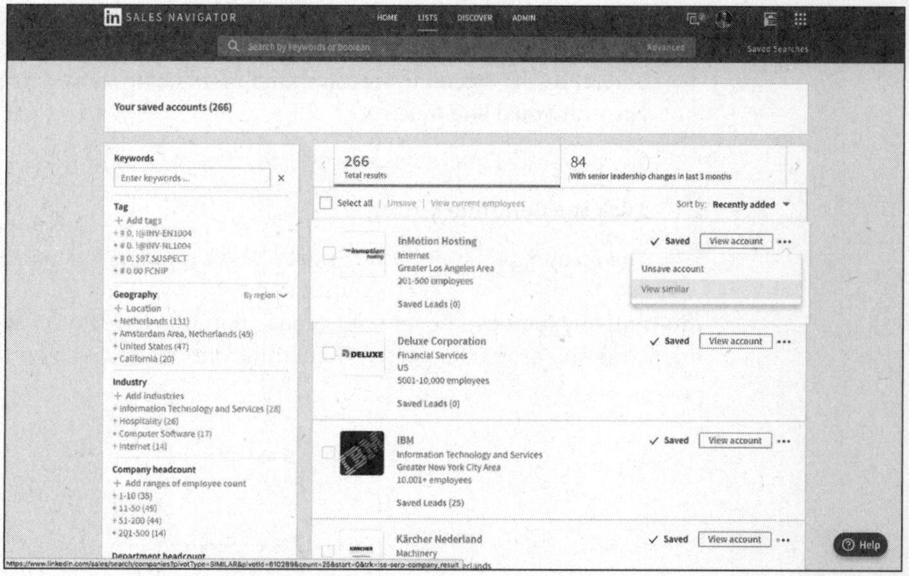

FIGURE 6-11:
Sales Navigator suggests similar accounts for you to save.

TIP

Once you're on the View Similar page, if you hover your mouse pointer over the three-dot icon again (next to any of the entries) and select the View Similar option, the page will refresh with even more companies that fit your criteria.

PRO TIP: SAVING YOUR COMPANY, COLLEAGUES, AND COMPETITORS

It's always a good idea to treat your own company, colleagues, and competitors the way you treat leads and accounts. In other words, save and tag their accounts, look up and save employees as leads, and keep an eye on their updates in your feed. You never know what kind of information you may stumble upon that you wouldn't have known otherwise.

For example, maybe a colleague in a different department ended up leaving the company. Since you have him saved as a lead, when he changes his employment information on his LinkedIn profile, you will see that specific update in your feed. Where he was once a colleague on the same team, now he may be a bona fide lead. And keeping an eye on your competition? That should be a no-brainer!

3

Engaging with Leads

Chapter **7**

Becoming Top of Mind with Your Leads

Y ou've put the time in. You've laid the groundwork. It's time to really get down to the business of social selling. Now is the time you start pounding the pavement (metaphorically speaking, of course), and start interacting and engaging with the leads you've painstakingly collected. If you've followed all (or at least most) of my advice thus far, you're more than ready to take your social-selling game to the next level.

In this chapter, I go into the nuts and bolts of how to engage with your leads on a regular basis to become and stay top of mind. I also show you how to narrow down the leads available to you in LinkedIn Sales Navigator into more tailored lists that produce results faster. Finally, I jump into the specifics of a great tool for interacting with leads that's included with certain Team-level and Enterprise-level Sales Navigator plans: PointDrive.

Engaging with Leads

As I discuss in Chapter 1, social selling is about making connections with people first. The idea is that over time, you will build up enough of a network of potential sales through your use of social media that an increase in sales is the natural result of these efforts. People want to buy from people they like. And people begin to like other people when they get to know them first.

Sales Navigator is a great tool to grow your network, and it has a number of helpful options to facilitate that growth. The "social" part is up to you, though. You have to be social to succeed in social selling, and how else are you going to be social if you don't engage with the leads you collect in Sales Navigator?

In the context of social networking, *engaging* can mean a few different things. You can use one of the provided buttons to "like" or otherwise show your appreciation for a person's content, you can share others' content using one of the network's methods, or you can take the time to write a comment. There is a time and a place for each of those options.

TIP

A good rule of thumb is that the more time you spend engaging with a lead by using a social network's option, the better your chances for catching that lead's attention. In other words, taking the time to write a thoughtful comment holds more weight than clicking the "thumbs up" button.

Interacting with top updates

When you first log into Sales Navigator, you are taken to the updates feed on the home page, which, coincidently, is where you have your first opportunity to engage with your leads (see Figure 7-1). The updates feed lists the top updates from your saved leads and accounts.

Sales Navigator selects which top updates to show you based on your activity within the platform. For example, if you've been performing a lot of account searches within a particular industry, Sales Navigator shows you more updates from those companies, including information such as whether those companies are experiencing high headcount growth in the past year.

If there's a post from a lead in your feed, you can click the "You and <Name>" link at the bottom of that update to see any connections or commonalities between you and that person. In Figure 7-1, you see that Doris and I both belong to the LinkedIn Group called "Digital Marketing" and we share 15 connections in common.

When a lead's update or updates appear in your feed, you're given the option to "like" the update, comment on it, or both. I recommend you do both and here's why: Clicking the "like" button on a person's update is mindless. You technically don't even have to had read the update to do so. It takes virtually zero effort, though it does show a tiny bit of acknowledgement to the person making the post.

FIGURE 7-1:
When you log into Sales Navigator, you see the top updates from leads and accounts first.

Click to see what you and this contact have in common

When you both "like" the update and leave a comment, you're still showing that appreciation, but you're also taking it a step further by taking the time to write a comment pertaining to the update. Just make sure the comment is actually related to the update. Nothing screams "lazy" like someone who simply adds a "thanks!" or a "nice story!" comment to an update.

TIP

Take the time to add details, such as mentioning why you liked the article or a short personal anecdote related to the topic. People love to know that you've actually put time and effort into engaging with their updates.

When a person shares more than one update within a 24-hour period, the last two updates appear in the feed, like you see in Figure 7-2 with my connection, Brian. This is helpful for a couple of different reasons. First, you know that the individual is active on LinkedIn, so he or she is more likely to receive any messages you send within a reasonable amount of time. Second, what that person posts may give you insight into what's important in his or her life and/or career at the moment. And as with the single update shown in Figure 7-1, the double-update box contains information about how you and that person are connected.

TIP

If a person hasn't posted an update on LinkedIn in over 30 days, chances are good he or she just doesn't sign into the site all that often. I recommend moving your attention elsewhere.

Click to send this contact a message

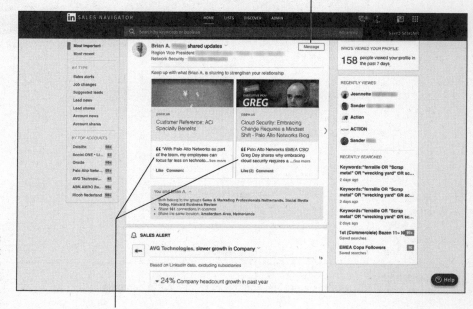

Grouped updates

Interacting with recent updates

The default view for the updates feed is to show the most important updates. You can, however, filter the results to show only the most recent updates by clicking the "Most recent" link in the Filter Your Updates box that appears in the left column of the home page. Once you do that, all the updates you see will be in chronological order with the newest on top. While this a good way to get up to date quickly on the latest updates from your network, you may have to do a lot of scrolling if you're looking for anything in particular.

What's helpful about sorting your results like this is that the most recent updates are grouped together by account, with any saved leads who work at that company below the company's updates. This is useful because you have company news front and center. If you decide to reach out to your lead regarding the company update (and you are, right?), you don't have to search high and low for it. You simply click the "Message" button that appears to the right of the lead's name and you can contact the lead right then and there. You can, of course, "like" and comment on these updates as well.

Sorting Updates by Type

In the Filter Your Updates box that appears in the left column of the Sales Navigator home page are seven filtering options:

> » Sales alerts

> » Job changes

> » Suggested leads

> » Lead news

> » Lead shares

> » Account news

> » Account shares

Let's take a look at these in more detail.

Sales alerts

The first filtering option in the Filter Your Results box filters your updates to show only the sales alerts from the accounts you follow (see Figure 7-3). When you filter your search results using this method, you go from seeing updates from both leads and accounts, regardless of what the updates are, to seeing only sales alerts.

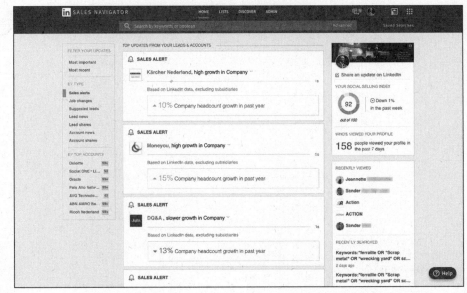

FIGURE 7-3:
Filter your updates to see only sales alerts.

Sales alerts for accounts show what the hiring trends are for the companies in question. For example, in Figure 7-3, you see that the second company in the list, Moneyou, has been experiencing high growth with a 15 percent rise in headcount in the past year.

Knowing when a company is doing more hiring or cutting back is a good indicator of how well the company is doing financially. If a company is adding a number of people in a short amount of time, that means it's experiencing a rise in sales and revenue. What does that mean for me, you ask? Well, it means not only the possibility of more sales opportunities in the future, but also the ability to grow your social network even more.

REMEMBER

On the flip side, if a company is laying people off or is under a hiring freeze, that could signify the company's sales have slowed or decreased over the past year. If this was a company that you've had your sights on as a lead, you may want to look elsewhere.

Job changes

Figure 7-4 shows my top updates sorted by which leads made a job change in the past 90 days. In addition to seeing what the lead's new roll is and at which company, Sales Navigator also tells you how you and that person are connected.

TOP UPDATES FROM YOUR LEADS & ACCOUNTS

Simon ▓▓ had a job change ⌄
Director · ▓▓▓▓▓▓▓▓▓▓▓▓

Message

2d

Reach out to see how you can support Simon in the new role

New role:
Director at ▓▓▓▓▓▓▓▓▓▓▓

You and Simon ⌄
- Both belong to the group **Harvard Business Review**
- Share 2 connections in common

Emily ▓▓ had a job change ⌄
Demand Generation Manager & Internal Marketo Consultant [FTC] ·
▓▓▓▓▓▓▓▓

Message

9d

Reach out to see how you can support Emily in the new role

New role:
Demand Generation Manager & Internal Marketo Consultant [FTC] at ▓▓▓▓▓▓▓▓▓

You and Emily ⌄
- Both belong to the group **Digital Marketing**
- Share 2 connections in common

Aviel ▓▓ had a job change ⌄
Senior Consultant | Solution 49x · ▓▓▓▓▓▓▓

Message

9d

Reach out to see how you can support Aviel in the new role

FIGURE 7-4:
These leads have had a job change in the past three months.

For example, in Figure 7-4, Simon recently became a director at Thorpebird Consulting. Under the "You and Simon" section, I see that we have two connections in common and that we're both members of the Harvard Business Review group.

In addition to giving me a reason to message him to congratulate him on his new job, I can also strike up a conversation about something that was recently posted in our shared group. Just by using this filter, I'm presented with three different ways to build a rapport with Simon.

Suggested leads

The third filter in the Filter Your Updates list is Suggested leads, which is shown in Figure 7-5. Apply this filter to see updates from only those leads Sales Navigator recommends you follow. Sales Navigator determines who to suggest based on your activity and the sales preferences you set when you opened your account. (Sales preferences are discussed in detail in Chapter 5.) You can change those preferences at any time by hovering your mouse pointer over your profile photo in the main navigation menu bar at the top of your screen and selecting Settings from the drop-down menu that appears. Once you do that, Sales Navigator recommends leads based on those new settings. The leads you've already saved from previous recommendations, however, remain.

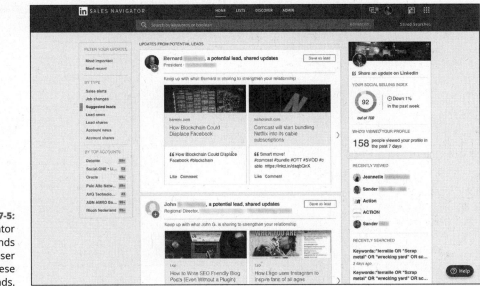

FIGURE 7-5:
Sales Navigator recommends you take a closer look at these possible leads.

The usefulness of this filter option should be pretty obvious: It's a great way to take advantage of the LinkedIn data Sales Navigator utilizes when picking out the leads it thinks you'll find the most useful. In other words, Sales Navigator is doing the heavy lifting for you! You can take advantage of its hard work with one click of your mouse.

Lead news

Lead news, the filter shown in Figure 7-6, is the filter to use when you're looking for general information about your leads, such as whether any leads recently changed jobs or had a work anniversary. As with the other filtering and sorting options, there is a section underneath each lead that lists what you and this lead have in common, such as how many mutual connections you have and whether you are both members of the same groups.

The Lead news filter is similar to the Job changes filter, so you can use it in the same way: Reach out to the person to congratulate him or her on the new job or otherwise acknowledge the news and strike up a conversation about a mutual connection or a group you're both a member of. It's a great way to break the ice because everyone wants their victories to be recognized.

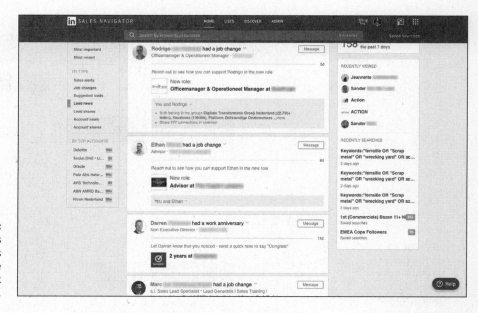

FIGURE 7-6:
This filter shows you which leads had a job change or a work anniversary.

Lead shares

So what types of updates are your leads posting on their LinkedIn accounts? The Lead shares filter (Figure 7-7) gives you exactly that information. Whether your leads are posting an article or a simple text-only update, you can stay up to date on what topics are of interest enough to your leads to post on their LinkedIn profiles.

Using this filter gives you the opportunity to increase your engagement with people you have already classified as leads. You can "like" and comment on their updates, showing that you're paying attention to them, their careers, and their interests. They'll be more open to communicating one-on-one with you if you take the time to reach out about something other than your own product or service.

FIGURE 7-7:
What are your leads sharing on LinkedIn?

Account news

The Account news filter shown in Figure 7-8 is similar to the Lead news filter except that it pertains to the companies you follow as opposed to the people. The biggest difference is that for account news, it typically means when your saved accounts are literally *in the news*.

Why could this be helpful for you and your social-selling activities? There are a couple of different reasons. First, if the news is positive and financials-related, that could mean the company is in the market for your product or service. For example, did the company get additional venture capital funding? Was it awarded a large contract? Both of these events could mean that projects that may have been shelved for a lack of funding may be picked up and dusted off.

REMEMBER

A helpful feature of the Account news filter is that Sales Navigator tells you which of your saved leads works at this particular company. So not only do you have the news about the company, but also you have an "in" with this lead. It's almost as valuable as specific news about the lead!

TIP

I recommend you save your competitors as leads simply to keep an eye on any news that comes out about them. It never hurts to keep up on what's happening in their worlds.

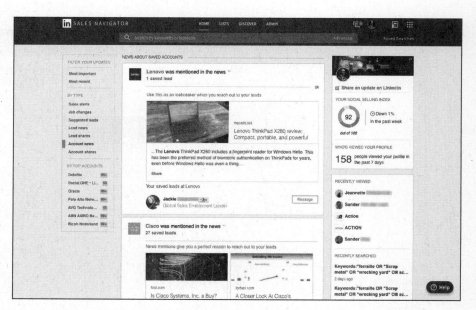

FIGURE 7-8:
Extra! Extra! Read all about your saved accounts' news.

Account shares

As with the Lead shares filter, the Account shares filter shown in Figure 7-9 shows you what your accounts have been posting on their LinkedIn profiles. When an account you've saved posts an update, more often than not it's news about the company itself or the industry. If it's the former, you should consider reaching out to any connections you have at the company to offer congratulations (or regrets, depending on the news).

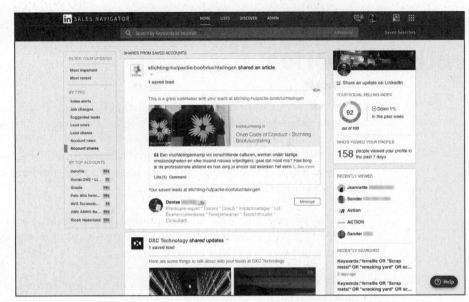

FIGURE 7-9:
What are your
saved accounts
sharing on
LinkedIn?

If the update is something industry-related, here's your chance to stay abreast on what's up and coming in the world of your prospect! Maybe it'll spur some ideas into other companies or industries that you may want to consider targeting.

As with Account news, if you have any saved leads who work at this company, those people are listed underneath the update along with anything you have in common, including shared connections and groups.

Top accounts

Underneath the Filter Your Updates box in the left column of the Sales Navigator home page is a section titled "By Top Accounts." It lists the accounts you encounter the most on LinkedIn. By *encounter* I mean not only do you engage with these companies the most by "liking" and commenting on their updates or the updates of their employees you have saved as leads, but also how frequently these companies show up in search results based on criteria you input.

If you refer back to Figure 7-9, you see that a couple of my top accounts are Deloitte and Oracle, both of which have over 99 updates that I have to catch up on! While Deloitte and Oracle aren't the focus of my social-selling activities at the moment (hence me not viewing all their updates), they are companies I'm interested in keeping an eye on for one reason or another. If the time comes when I want to either find out some information about them or gather some intel on a lead of mine who works there, I know exactly where to go.

Creating and Managing Content with PointDrive

PointDrive is a feature of Sales Navigator that is included with some Team-level and Enterprise-level plans. It allows you to create, store, and manage presentations that are then packaged up to be sent to leads. PointDrive presentations can be personalized with your company's branding and contact information, making it a great option when you want to send prospects more information in a professional-looking manner.

Typically, when people send anyone content, that content is sent as attachments to an email message. Most of the time those emails contain long explanations and descriptions about what that content entails.

Besides being inconvenient for the recipient, the problem with this method of information delivery is that typically no one person is responsible for purchasing decisions in companies anymore. Often a committee is involved. It's then up to the original recipient to forward the email and attachments. The accompanying messages may get lost in the shuffle, and things can quickly get confusing. This is what PointDrive sets out to avoid.

REMEMBER

Instead of having to open a number of attachments in an email message, leads just click the PointDrive link you send them. It really couldn't be any easier or more straight-forward.

Creating presentations

How does one go about using PointDrive to create professional-looking content? Follow these steps:

1. **From any page in Sales Navigator, navigate to PointDrive by clicking the grid icon in the main navigation menu bar and selecting the PointDrive option.**

   You are taken to your PointDrive home page, similar to the page you see in Figure 7-10.

2. **Click the New Presentation button that appears in the top-right corner of the screen underneath your profile photo.**

   The screen showing a blank presentation template appears, as shown in Figure 7-11.

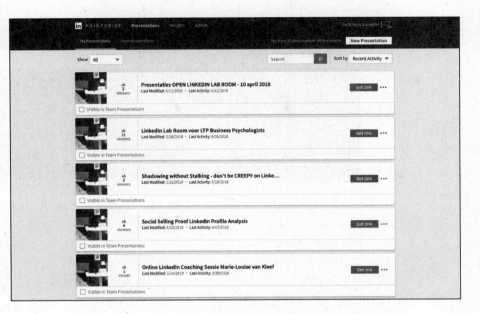

FIGURE 7-10:
The PointDrive
home page
after adding
presentations.

3. **To add your first piece of content, click the Insert Content button.**

A new page appears where you can decide on the type of content you want to add (see Figure 7-12). This content module is also called an *asset*. You can add a file, link, video, or map.

4. **Click to select whatever option applies to the content you want to create.**

If you are uploading a file, you can pull it from your computer or a cloud-storage solution such as OneDrive, Dropbox, or Box.

5. **Customize the presentation by adding a title, changing the colors, and/or adding a personalized message that is sent to the lead along with the link to the presentation.**

TIP

You should always add a personalized message to your presentation. It serves as a reminder about who you are and what type of information the recipient is about to view.

6. **(Optional) If you want to add more content (assets), click the "+Add New Entry" button underneath the file selection box.**

TIP

I recommend adding no more than four or five pieces of content at a time to keep the presentation a reasonable length. You don't want to annoy your lead by sending hundreds of pages of content!

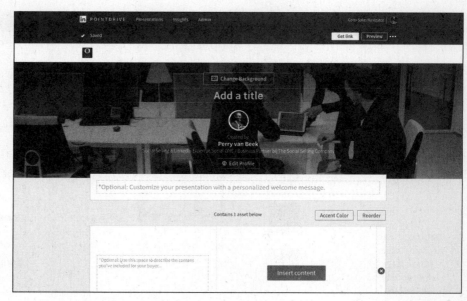

FIGURE 7-11:
Start creating
a new
presentation.

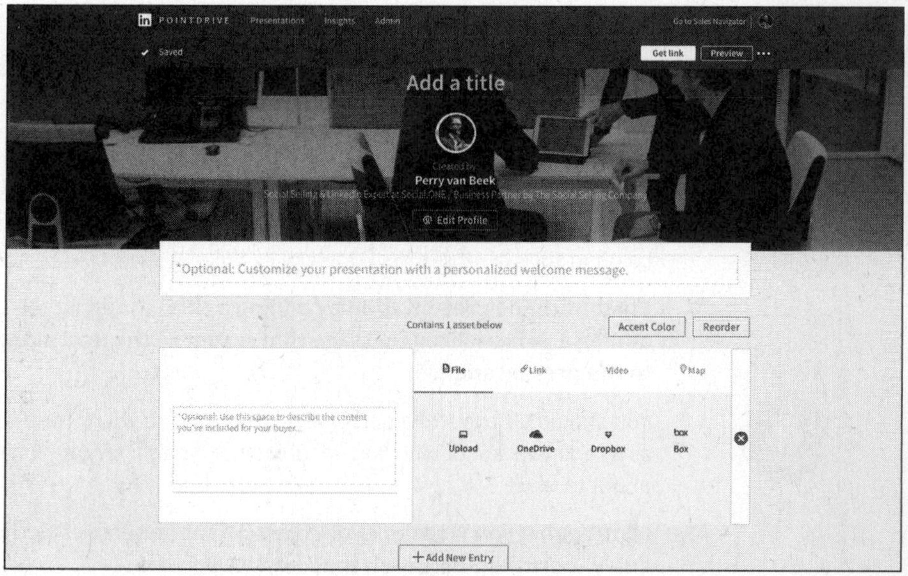

FIGURE 7-12:
Adding assets
to your new
presentation.

7. **Click the Preview button in the top-right corner of the screen (refer to Figure 7-12).**

   You should always preview your content before sending it out to ensure it looks professional and how you intend it to look.

8. **If all looks well, click the Get Link button.**

   The Get Link button is next to the Preview button in the top-right corner of the screen. When clicked, Sales Navigator generates a link to the presentation that can be shared through email or InMail messages.

Viewing team members' presentations

PointDrive is a shared option, so everyone on your Sales Navigator Team or Enterprise account can use it to create and send content.

By default, your own presentations are private; however, you can click the check box that says "Visible in Team Presentations" underneath each presentation's thumbnail on your PointDrive home page to let other team members access it on the Team Presentations page. For example, there may be times when a team member wants an extra set of eyes on a presentation he or she created. To access a team member's page, click the Team Presentations link located on the left side of your PointDrive home page underneath the top menu bar. Once clicked, you see a screen like the one shown in Figure 7-13.

If you find that your team isn't making the best use of PointDrive, you can shut off access to it through your Sales Navigator Admin Settings page.

With the Team-level Sales Navigator plan, LinkedIn only grants you ten PointDrive presentations per month. If you haven't used them all by the end of the month, you'll lose those unused slots on the first of every month. To avoid that, simply set a reminder in your calendar toward the end of the month to save the unused PointDrive presentations. What I recommend you do is click the New Presentation button and then changing the title to "Placeholder." This automatically saves the presentation and I can then change the title later when I run of of PointDrive slots.

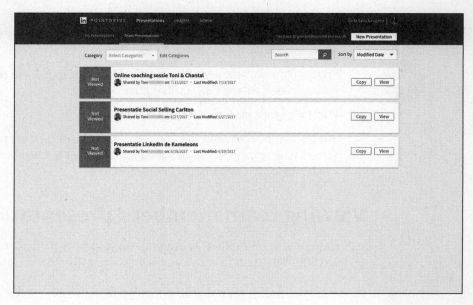

FIGURE 7-13:
View other team
members'
presentations
here.

Tracking customer interactions

When leads click the unique PointDrive link you provide them, they're taken to your presentation. On the back end, Sales Navigator collects valuable data about when leads view and interact with your presentation that it calls *PointDrive Insights*.

PointDrive Insights give you the following information about the viewers of your presentations:

>> The number of times a lead clicked your PointDrive link

>> The amount of time the lead spent viewing the presentation

>> The time of day the presentation was accessed

>> The location where the lead viewed the presentation based on IP address

>> Whether the person viewed the presentation on a computer or a mobile device

>> The browser type used by the person to view the presentation

To view the PointDrive Insights of your presentations at any time, simply click the Insights link that appears in the top menu bar to see a screen like the one shown in Figure 7-14. On this page, you can see every time a lead views a presentation, broken down by date.

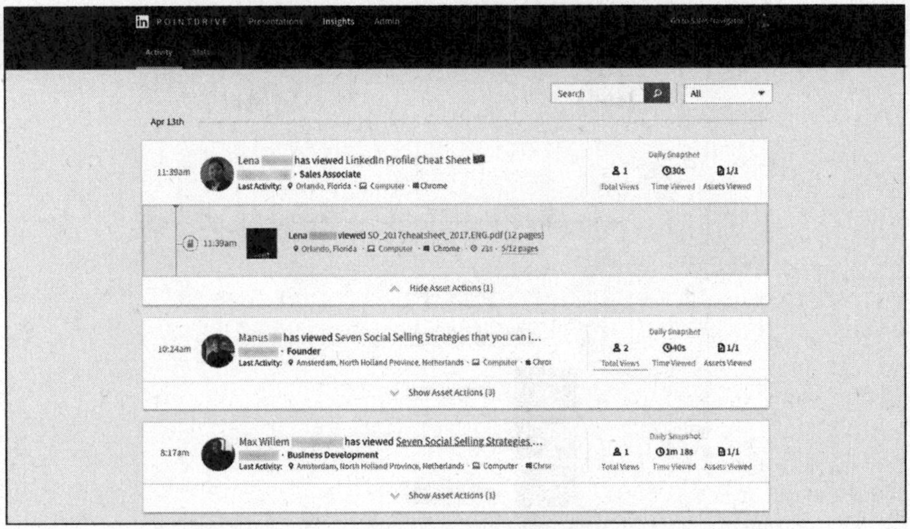

FIGURE 7-14:
These leads viewed my presentations.

If you click the Stats link that appears to the right of the Activity link (on the left side beneath the top menu bar), you're taken to a screen similar to the one shown in Figure 7-15. This Stats page gives you a quick look into your PointDrive usage by showing you the number of presentations you've created and which content received the most views.

TIP

It's important to keep abreast on what presentations are performing the best so you can continue to use that one and maybe review and revise ones that aren't such high performers. Furthermore, taking a regular look at PointDrive Insights can give you a good idea into who has taken an interest in your product or service. If you see that certain leads watch it straight through multiple times, chances are good they like what they see!

REMEMBER

Keep track of who views your presentations because you should follow up with them shortly afterward.

FIGURE 7-15:
A quick snapshot of your PointDrive stats.

PRO TIP: SHARING PREQUALIFIED LEADS

There's going to come a point in time when, for whatever reason, the lead you were pursuing turns out to not be a qualified lead for you. This prospect has a pain point (or points) and did his or her research, and you've nurtured this lead and moved the lead through the sales cycle. But then all of a sudden, the company changes direction (for example) and the lead is no longer applicable to your division.

Instead of writing off this lead, you should always pass leads along to a colleague who is able to handle the customer's needs. Not only will your colleague be grateful for the pre-qualified lead, but also the customer will be thankful that you didn't leave them hanging simply because you weren't going to get a sale out of them. You never know, this colleague may be in the same position one day, and your name will be at the top of the list when he or she is looking to pass on a prequalified lead.

Chapter **8**

Connecting with Leads

You can have the fanciest, shiniest, and best social-selling tools in the world, but if you don't make connections with people, you're never going to be able to call them leads. The good news is that because LinkedIn is a social network, everyone else on the site is there to meet others as well. Now, making connections with prospects just comes down to the best ways to initiate contact.

For many people, reaching out and making contact is the most difficult part of sales. But with social networks and the rise of social selling, people are generally more open to connecting with strangers — provided that the person isn't using heavy-handed, spammy sales tactics that make every legitimate, respectful sales professional cringe.

In this chapter, I give you some pointers on how to use LinkedIn Sales Navigator to establish a rapport with a prospect, including how to go about finding mutual interests to use as an icebreaker. I show you how to determine if you and your prospect have any mutual connections on LinkedIn, and if you're in any of the same LinkedIn Groups. Finally, I discuss some best practices of using InMail to approach potential leads.

Identifying Common Ground

Think about it. Who would you rather buy something from: someone with whom you had a lengthy discussion about your mutual love of the New York Yankees or someone who was all business all the time?

Assuming everything else was equal, you're most likely going to purchase something from the fellow Yankees fan. After all, you two built a *rapport*. In other words, you two found a common ground and you probably felt more comfortable with this person and maybe even trusted this person more than the other salesperson.

What it comes down to is people want to buy from people they know, like, and trust. Social media has made this a little more difficult, though. On social media, you don't have the benefit of being able to read body-language cues or facial expressions. If you say something to a prospect in person and then he or she looks uncomfortable, you know you've said something wrong. You can maybe back pedal or clarify what you really meant, if you think you were misunderstood.

Another benefit of meeting prospects in person is that you are able to receive visual clues to potential commonalities. For example, you may be able to see something the prospect has on his or her desk that relates to a shared hobby, or that he or she is wearing a T-shirt from your favorite vacation spot. You can then speak to these things to build rapport.

Checking mutual interests

You don't have the opportunity to pick up on many visual clues on social media because you're not face to face with the person, in the same room as that person, or perhaps not even in the same city as that person. All is not lost, though. There are still a few things you can do to try to build rapport with prospects, such as:

>> Look at their social network accounts (for example, their LinkedIn profiles) to see if you have anything in common, such as a past employer or alma mater.

>> Scan their posts to determine if you have anything to add to a conversation they've had or a comment they've made.

>> Say something casual on your own social network accounts and if anyone comments, try to keep that conversation going.

>> Ask a question on your social network accounts and see who responds. Strike up a conversation with those people.

TIP

Your attempts to make a connection with a prospect doesn't have to be a formal thing. In fact, the less formal you are, the better. They're called *social* networks for a reason. People want to know you're a real person with feelings and interests outside of selling them something. Be your friendly, outgoing self.

Pinpointing mutual connections

LinkedIn is all about networks and connections. It's like social media's version of the "six degrees of separation" concept, which theorizes that any two people in the world are six or fewer acquaintances apart. While LinkedIn only goes so far as third-degree connections, it's the same idea.

REMEMBER

The more people you connect with directly on LinkedIn (first-degree connections), the more your second- and third-degree network grows. This idea is one of the keys to success in social selling and luckily, LinkedIn makes it easy to make those connections. Well, it makes it easy to *find* potential connections. It's up to you to solidify them.

How do you go about seeing if you have any mutual connections with someone? LinkedIn will tell you, of course. If you have the name of a prospect in mind, use LinkedIn's search box at the top of your personal LinkedIn profile or your Sales Navigator account profile to see if you have any mutual connections. For example, in Figure 8-1, I typed a name into the search box at the top of my personal LinkedIn profile. As it turns out, there is only one Sarah with that last name, so right away I see that she is my second-degree connection. In other words, we have a first-degree connection in common.

FIGURE 8-1: Searching for a person from the search function on my personal profile.

When I select her name from that drop-down menu, I'm taken to Sarah's full profile page, which is shown in Figure 8-2. On that screen, I see that our mutual connection is a woman named Michelle. At that point, I can decide if I have enough of a relationship with Michelle to feel comfortable asking her for an introduction to Sarah. If I do, I click the link that says "1 Mutual Connection," where I am given the option to send Michelle a message asking her to make the introduction (see Figure 8-3).

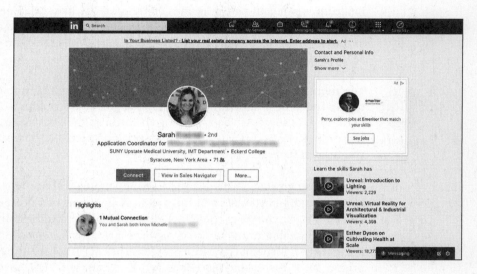

FIGURE 8-2: Determining what connection we have in common.

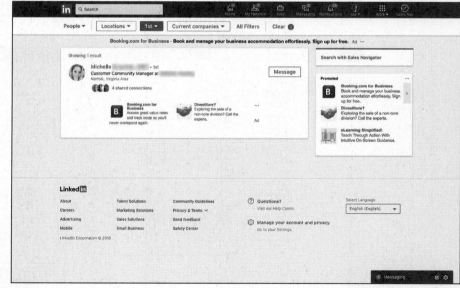

FIGURE 8-3: I'm given the opportunity to send Michelle a message.

Doing that same search in Sales Navigator also brings up Sarah's name and the fact that we are second-degree connections in the suggested results drop-down menu. When I select that result, I see the screen shown in Figure 8-4.

One of the big differences between the two search options is the Save as Lead button that appears on the right side of Sarah's profile in the search results box in Sales Navigator. Clicking this button means you will start to follow all of Sarah's LinkedIn activity, including work anniversaries, job changes, and other updates she posts. This activity shows up on your Sales Navigator update feed, which I discuss in detail in Chapter 4. I am not given the option to save Sarah as a lead if I conduct the search from my LinkedIn profile.

This sounds like the type of information you see when you become a first-degree connection to someone, doesn't it? It sure is, except with Sales Navigator, you don't have to be a first-degree connection to see that person's updates, and Sarah is not notified that you've added her as a lead. This is a great way to get an idea about what she's been up to, even maybe giving you some information to use when it comes time to reach out and make a connection request to her (or when asking for an introduction from one of your first-degree connections).

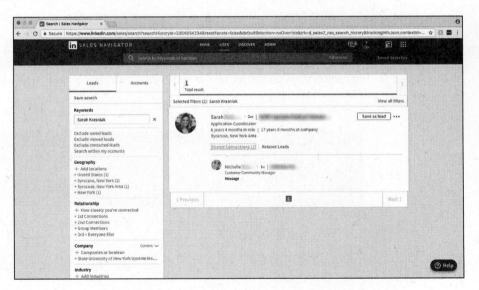

FIGURE 8-4: Search results in Sales Navigator.

TIP

If you have a Team- or Enterprise-level Sales Navigator plan and thus have the TeamLink feature at your disposal, you should conduct your searches for potential leads from the Sales Navigator interface. With TeamLink, you can open up your network considerably. (See Chapter 1 for more information about viewing profiles and conducting searches with TeamLink.)

Determining mutual groups

Another way to connect with leads is through the LinkedIn Groups you belong to. The Groups feature is not specific to Sales Navigator, so you can quickly access it from your personal LinkedIn profile. The Groups page is where you can see the groups you belong to as well as search for other groups that may be of interest to you. If you started your own LinkedIn Group, this is also where you manage the settings and activities for those.

To reach the LinkedIn Groups page, follow these steps:

1. **Navigate to your LinkedIn personal profile page.**

   This is the page you see when you first log into LinkedIn.

2. **On the right side of the top menu bar, click the Work (or More) icon, which looks like a grid with six squares.**

   A menu box appears with a number of options.

3. **Click the Groups button that appears in the top row of this menu box.**

   You are now on your Groups home page (see Figure 8-5), where you can view the activity for the groups you belong to, as well as manage the groups you've started and search for new groups to join.

TIP

If you stay logged into your LinkedIn account even after you close your Internet browser, you can just go to www.linkedin.com/groups to be taken directly to your Groups home page.

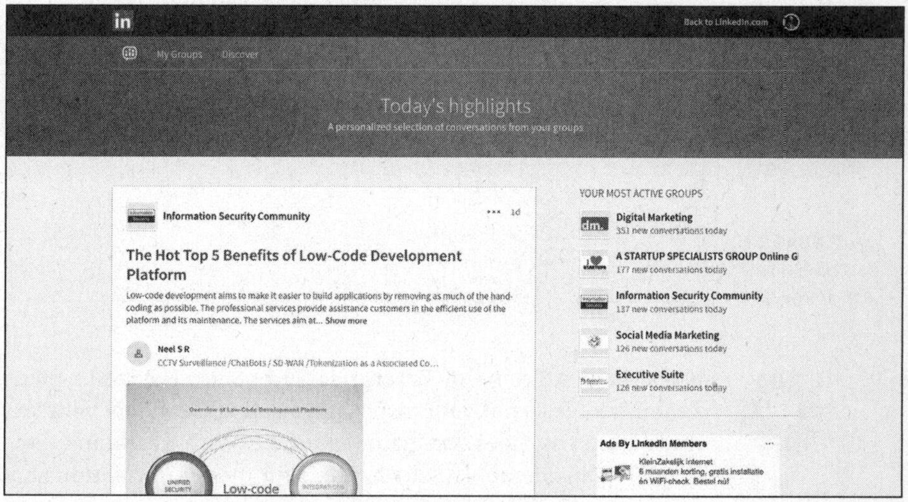

FIGURE 8-5:
The Groups home page is a great place to start when searching for a connection.

Once you're on your Groups home page, click the My Groups link that appears at the top left of the page to see a list of all the groups you belong to. Your groups are split up into two sections: The groups you manage are at the top and the groups you're a member of are underneath that.

When you click a group's name, you're taken to that group's home page. For example, when I click the link to the Digital Marketing group I am a member of, I am taken to its home page, as shown in Figure 8-6. On the right side of that page is the Members section that lists the number of members. Click that number and you're brought to the group membership list. The *searchable* group membership list, I might add. Do you see where I'm going with this? That's right; type your prospect's name into the search box on the right side that says "Find a Member . . .". As you type, LinkedIn suggests members in a list. Scroll down until you find your prospect. If you hover over the prospect's name, a box appears that gives you a snapshot of this person's profile, including what degree of connection you two share (see Figure 8-7).

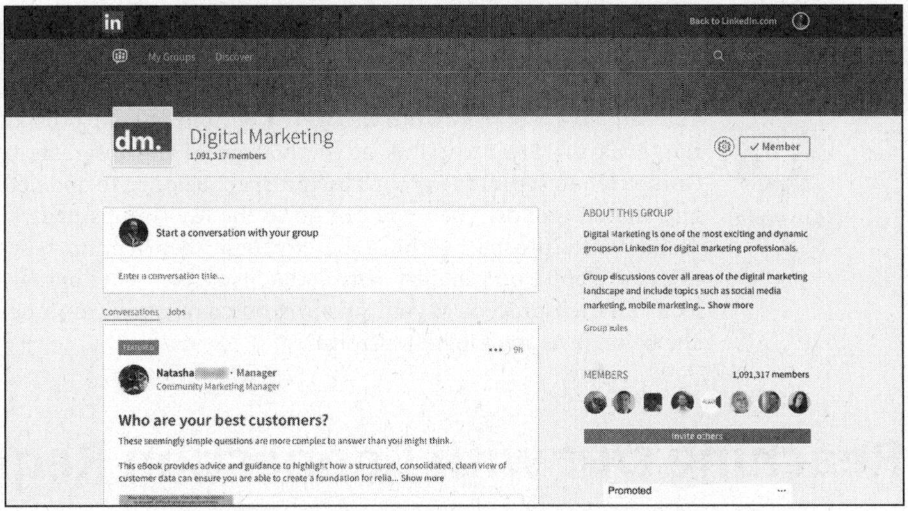

FIGURE 8-6:
A group's home page with the number of members listed on the right side.

Unfortunately, you cannot see any mutual connections in this snapshot, but you can always click the prospect's name or the View Profile button in the snapshot to visit the full profile. If you just want to cut to the chase and send a message, you can do that from this member list as well. Just click the Message icon that appears all the way to the right of the person's name.

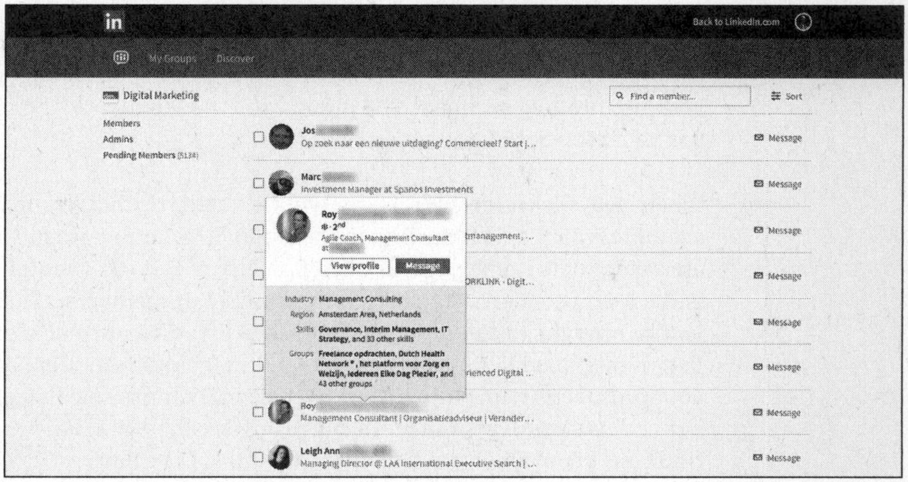

Figure depicting the Digital Marketing group member list with a hover profile snapshot.

FIGURE 8-7:
Hover over a name to see a snapshot of that prospect's profile.

TIP

You can message second- and third-degree connections from within the Groups you have in common, thus avoiding having to use up a valuable InMail credit. One thing to keep in mind, however, is that you can only send up to 15 of this type of message per month.

REMEMBER

You can always scroll all the way to the bottom of your prospect's LinkedIn profile, click the See More link at the bottom of the Interests box, then click the Groups tab to see all the groups the prospect belongs to and determine if you have any shared groups. Then you can go to the My Groups page on your profile and search for the prospect within a shared group. Keep in mind, however, that LinkedIn offers a Group icon visibility setting that users can set to opt out of showing Group icons on their profiles. If your prospect opted out, you won't be able to see if he or she belongs to any LinkedIn Groups.

Reaching Out with Connection Requests

You hear me say this over and over again throughout this book: LinkedIn is all about connections, so *make those connections!* In addition, if you're reading this book, chances are good you have a premium Sales Navigator account and are pretty familiar with LinkedIn itself as well as how to go about sending connection requests.

However, here's a quick refresher. To send a connection request, all you have to do is visit the prospect's LinkedIn profile and click the Connect button that appears underneath the person's profile picture, as shown in Figure 8-8.

Once you click the Connect button, you see a pop-up box like the one shown in Figure 8-9 that says that members are more likely to respond if you add a personalized note to your request. If you choose to do so, click the Add a Note button. If you don't want to add a note, click the Send Now button, which I only recommend if you know the person well.

Because this book is about social selling, I'd be remiss if I didn't say that it's highly recommended you include a personalized note when you request a connection. That way you can remind the person about how you know each other, for example. Or, if you've never met the person but have a connection in common, mention that person's name in your note. The point is, you should always write a note to accompany your connection requests because it's a great way to break the ice.

Approaching with InMail Messages

InMail messages are basically LinkedIn email messages. The good news with InMails is that you don't have to be a first-degree or even a second-degree connection to someone in order to send him or her an InMail. It's a great way to connect with prospects who are further out in your network. The bad news is the fact that you only get a certain number of InMail credits a month. The Professional-level Sales Navigator plan (the lowest level) gives you 20 InMails per month. The Team-level plan gives you 30, and the Enterprise-level plan gives you 50 InMails per month. (See Chapter 1 for more about what is included in each subscription plan.)

REMEMBER

These limits are put into place to prevent any overzealous sales professionals from bombarding other LinkedIn members with spam-like messages. While that's a good thing, it really puts a damper on sales folks like us who take our social-selling seriously.

You can send InMail to LinkedIn members in two different ways: via their profile pages or via search results you got in Sales Navigator. Now the caveat: If a LinkedIn member has set his or her privacy settings to not receive InMail messages, you can't send this person one by any of those options. But when you are able to send InMails to other LinkedIn users, the messages you send appear in your Sales Navigator inbox under the Pending tab, as shown on the left side of Figure 8-10. *Pending* means that the recipient has yet to see or open your message. Once they are opened, they move to the All Messages tab in your inbox.

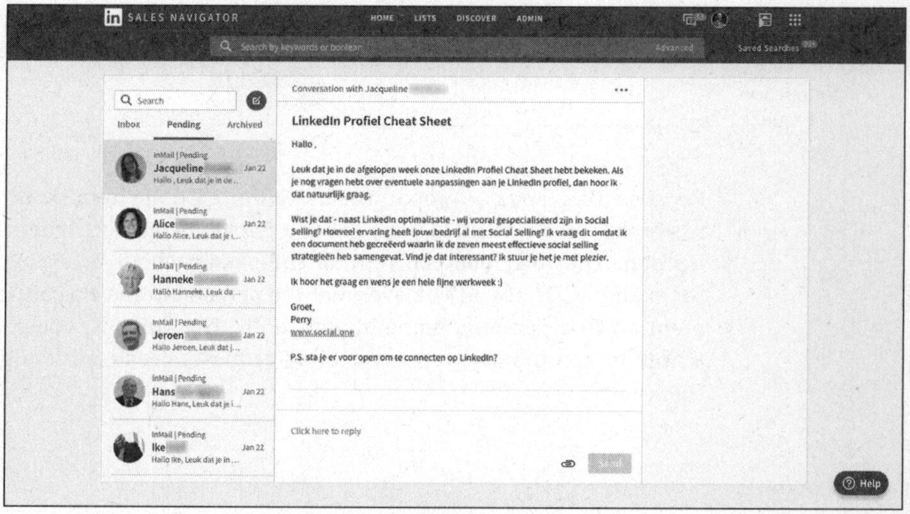

FIGURE 8-10:
Pending InMail messages are labeled as such and remain pending until opened.

TIP

I highly recommend you treat InMails like currency! Because you get a limited number, you should save them for individuals you cannot contact by any other means. For example, if you have a prospect who is active on another social network, try reaching out to that person via that platform first. A prospect who is not active on other social networks is the perfect recipient for a well-crafted, sincere InMail.

Here are some tips on writing InMails that get results:

>> **Take the time to personalize each message.** Let recipients see you've put effort into initiating contact with them and aren't just blasting out form messages to anyone and everyone.

>> **Write a compelling subject line to make the recipient want to open the message.** The subject line can make it or break it when it comes to your message being opened.

>> **Be concise and straightforward.** Chances are a recipient is only going to skim your message, so get to the point.

>> **Build a rapport.** Refer to the tips I offer about how to make a personal connection with recipients at the start of this chapter.

>> **Don't use overt, heavy-handed sales tactics.** This is social selling, so approach InMails like you approach other social media communication.

REMEMBER

There is a way that you can *technically* have an unlimited number of InMails. As long as the person you sent the InMail to responds, that InMail is credited back to your account. In other words, if you only have 30 InMails a month but you send 30 and all 30 responds in some way, you can continue to send InMails.

PRO TIP: TARGET OPEN PROFILES

Hunt the LIONs! No, I'm not advocating for you to sign up for an African safari. A LION is someone who is open to connecting on the site with just about anyone and everyone. It stands for *LinkedIn Open Networker,* and they're not always easy to spot.

Sometimes members have the acronym directly in their profiles, signaling to others that they are open to connecting, but others choose not to display the icon. It's a personal preference and you should choose what works for you and your social-selling goals.

I'm not recommending you to become a LION, but one of the benefits of connecting with LIONs is that your network will grow exponentially much quicker than if you stuck to the more traditional method of making connections on the site. Obviously, the larger your network, the larger the prospect pool. Sales Navigator is a robust tool and it's made for managing large networks.

Websites like www.opennetworker.com are dedicated to maintaining lists of LIONs and by joining, you have access to all the names of people on LinkedIn who are willing to connect with you. However, know that when you join any kind of LION site, you are opening yourself up to receiving a lot of spam. I don't recommend becoming a LION but if you do, I recommend signing up with an email address other than your main email account and then adding that email as a secondary one to your LinkedIn profile to avoid overcrowding your inbox.

4

Turning Leads into Valuable Relationships

Chapter 9

Developing a Daily Routine

B uilding your network — whether it's in person or on LinkedIn — takes time. Often people get discouraged because it's overwhelming to have to keep track of all the moving parts of social selling. If this sounds like you, well, today is your lucky day. I'm here to tell you that once you get up and running — once you have built up a network — you can start to spend a lot less hands-on time logged into LinkedIn Sales Navigator.

That's not to say you're not going to have to spend *any* time nurturing your sales activities. If that were the case, the world would be overrun with sales professionals, because who doesn't want to "set it and forget it"? What I'm here to tell you is that it doesn't have to take as much time as you think. In fact, I propose you spend just 30 minutes a day tending to your Sales Navigator activities. These 30 minutes can go a long way to staying on top of your social-selling game. In this chapter, I take you through the most important activities that, when you put just a few minutes a day into, can reap big rewards.

Achieving Social-Selling Success in 30 Minutes

Did you know that you can achieve social-selling success just by spending 30 minutes a day performing a few simple actions? You probably thought (or at least hoped) that the title of this section meant that I can teach you how to be a social-selling rock star in 30 minutes *total.* Believe me, if I could, I would! But social selling — and social media in general — just doesn't work like that.

A friend of mine is a social media marketing consultant. She works with small to medium-sized businesses helping them build their social media identities. I use the term *identities* because social media is more than just broadcasting content to your audience and hoping something sticks. If that sounds familiar, it's because that's what we've been doing for eons. Well, maybe not *that* long, but still, a long time. In fact, chances are, advertising has been around longer than you think.

Advertising in history

Allow me to take you back in time for a few minutes. There is a method to my madness, I promise. In 1704, the *Boston News-Letter* published the first advertisement, which was an announcement selling an estate in Oyster Bay on Long Island. Then in 1729, Benjamin Franklin got in on the advertising game and began publishing the *Pennsylvania Gazette* in Philadelphia, which contained an entire section of advertisements.

Skip ahead to 1843 when the first advertising agency started in Philadelphia. This was clearly a sign that advertisements were now a *thing.* Pennsylvania continued to lead the pack when the first radio station started in Pittsburgh in 1920. Two years later, ads started appearing on the radio. The first TV ads started airing in 1941. Then fast-forward to 1999 when the Internet advertising industry brought in over $2 billion in revenue.

TIP

If you want a wonderfully exhaustive timeline of the life of advertising, check out this AdAge article: `http://adage.com/article/special-report-the-advertising-century/ad-age-advertising-century-timeline/143661`.

What did I intend to illustrate with that warp-speed rundown of the growth of advertising? For starters, the fact that advertising has been around for a very (very) long time. People have been selling to people seemingly forever. (I'm exaggerating obviously, but c'mon, *1704!?*) When something has been around for that long, it's likely undergone many iterations. Mistakes were made and learned from (in theory), successes were replicated, and advancements in technology led to new delivery methods. We learned a lot about advertising and sales and how to present information to our audiences. That period of time laid the groundwork for advertising practices that are still in effect today, albeit some of them have been tweaked over the years.

But there was a period of nearly 60 years when advertising technology didn't change all that much. Once TV advertising entered the picture, it became the pinnacle of the ad world; something large companies readily took advantage of and something small companies wished they could take advantage of.

All of those advertising methods had one thing in common, however. Each method is a one-way conversation. The audience is presented with the advertisement, either via radio, TV, or in a print ad, and that was that. Advertisers had little control over what happened after consumers received the ad, as they weren't in the minds of the people, so to speak. Advertisers didn't have boots on the ground in the moments their content was consumed.

Enter social media and a whole new world of possibilities.

The social media game changer

Social media is a two-way conversation. It connects not only people around the word, but also connects companies with the very individuals who consume their products and services. The access consumers have to companies is unprecedented. Where getting ahold of customer service once meant calling a dedicated toll-free number, now all we have to do is send out a tweet or post a question to a company's Facebook page. If a company is doing "social" correctly, you'll get a response quickly.

There was a period of time when using social media for sales was frowned upon. And it still is, in a way. Whereas overt, heavy-handed selling is frowned upon, using the networks you build on social platforms like LinkedIn has become common practice. After all, social media is about *networking,* and sales is about *networking,* so it makes sense that the two can go together like bread and butter. Or peanut butter and jelly. Or chips and salsa. Or — you get the idea.

Okay, now that you know how we got to where we are today in sales and advertising, it's time to get into how you can "get with the times" and spend just 30 minutes a day incorporating Sales Navigator into your everyday sales schedule.

Tracking Your Saved Leads and Accounts

For this first task, I recommend you spend just 12 minutes of your day tracking your saved leads and accounts. In Chapter 6, I discuss how to save leads and accounts. Here is where I tell you the importance of doing so. In Figure 9-1 you see the main landing page for my saved leads. In Figure 9-2 you see the landing page for my saved accounts.

Notice in Figure 9-1 the numerous ways to sort these leads in the left-hand column. What's important to keep a daily eye on are the Sales Spotlights that appear above the search results. (I talk about sorting, filtering, and Sales Spotlights in more detail in Chapter 5.) By clicking through these filtering options, you're able to see specific information about your leads, such as:

>> Which leads have changed jobs within the past 90 days (and what their new companies and positions are)

>> Whether there is a TeamLink intro available to you

>> Whether any leads were mentioned in the news in the past 30 days

>> Whether leads posted on LinkedIn in the past 30 days (indicating they're active users)

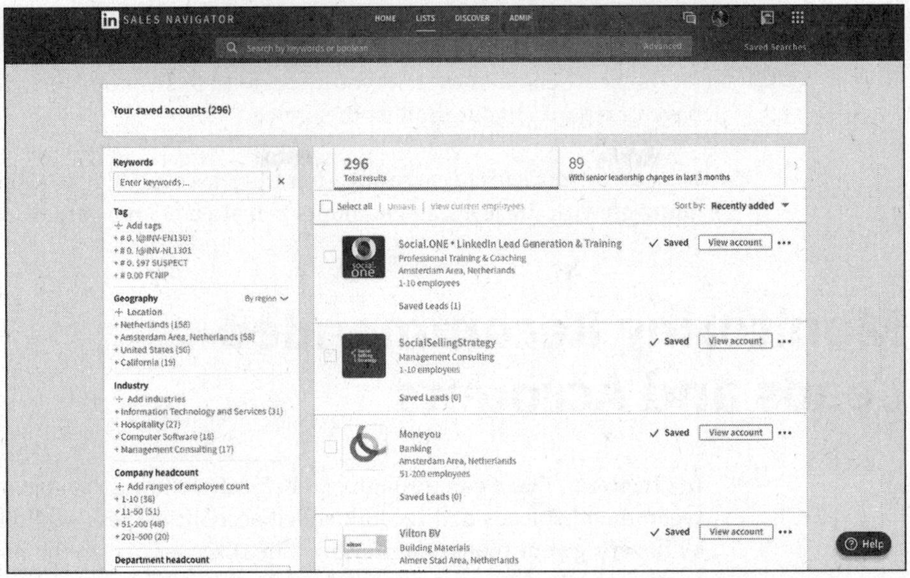

FIGURE 9-2: This page shows some of the accounts I've saved.

>> Whether you have any shared experiences (to help establish rapport)

>> Whether any leads follow your company on LinkedIn (possibly indicating an interest in working with you)

The Sales Spotlights section of the leads landing page is essentially a one-stop shop of information that you can use to connect with an individual and it changes frequently. Besides, you never know when a situation may arise when you get word that a person or company is in the market for your product. Checking this section on a daily basis may hold the key to striking up a conversation with that person.

REMEMBER

People buy from people they know, like, and trust, so be sure to utilize your shared experiences as much as you can!

In Figure 9-2, you see the landing page of my saved accounts. At the top of the list the only Sales Spotlight option is to filter by companies who have had a leadership change in the last three months. Why is this information useful and why should you check it out on a daily basis? Because you never know what happens in a company when there is a "change of guard." Often new management means new (or stalled) initiatives, and it's good to know what kind of situation you're walking into. For example, you may have had a great relationship with the manager of a particular department, but the new leader who is her replacement may not be on board with doing business with your company. On the flip side, when you see that there is new management, you have the perfect opportunity to reach out to this individual and introduce yourself.

If you had a relationship with the previous manager, be sure to mention that and let the new person know that you're there to answer any questions he or she may have in regard to your product or service.

It's not, too difficult to carve out a few minutes every day to keep abreast of what's going on with the leads and accounts you already know are worth your time, is it?

Monitoring Recommended Leads and Accounts

In Chapter 6, I take you through two helpful sections provided by Sales Navigator: recommended leads and recommended accounts. These sections can be accessed by hovering your mouse pointer over the Discover link in the main navigation bar at the top of your screen and selecting either Recommended Leads or Recommended Accounts from the drop-down menu that appears.

Let's start with recommended leads (see Figure 9-3). If you look at the top of the list of recommended leads, you see that this page has the same Sales Spotlight categories as the Saved Leads page shown earlier in Figure 9-1. The idea is that you will likely find viable leads from this list when you sort them using the Sales Spotlight options. Sales Navigator makes it easy to save these leads by providing a "Save as Lead" button to the right of the person's entry. All you have to do to save a recommended lead is click this button and that person is added to your saved leads. One addition to this option, however, is a small "X" that appears to the right of the Save as Lead button. This option lets you dismiss that lead.

Once you dismiss a lead by clicking the "X" next to that person's entry, Sales Navigator never shows you that person again, so make sure it really is someone you won't want to contact in the future.

As with the Saved Leads page, you can filter these results by selecting one of the options on the left side of the page such as Geography, Company Headcount, Seniority Level, and so on. When you sort by one (or more) of these filters, the number of people shown in the "Total Results" section in the Sales Spotlight bar lowers.

The more filters you apply, the fewer results you're shown. While that can be helpful in homing in on the perfect leads, you may also be missing out on great ones you wouldn't have normally considered.

FIGURE 9-3:
These are the
suggested leads
I keep an eye on.

How does Sales Navigator determine who to suggest, you ask? Sales Navigator (or rather, its algorithms) bases its recommendations on your activity and the Sales Preferences you set when you opened your account. (Sales Preferences are discussed in detail in Chapter 5.) You can change those preferences at any time by hovering your mouse pointer over your profile picture that appears in the main navigation bar at the top of your screen and selecting Settings from the drop-down menu. Once you do that, Sales Navigator begins recommending leads based on those new settings. The leads you've already saved from previous recommendations, however, remain.

The recommended accounts page (see Figure 9-4) looks similar to the recommended leads page shown in Figure 9-3; however, instead of a Save as Lead button, a Save as Account button appears to the right of the account name. In addition, the Sales Spotlight categories that appear at the top of the search results are the same as those that appear at the top of the Saved Accounts page discussed in Chapter 6. As a reminder, the options are limited to breaking the list down to only show companies (accounts) who have had a change in leadership in the last three months. The filtering options on the left side of the screen are the same as the Saved Accounts page as well.

I think it goes without saying why it's important to monitor the recommended accounts and leads pages closely (although I'm going to say it anyway). These search results are essentially "gimmies." They're potential leads that you don't have to perform searches to find. Sometimes you just don't have the time to perform full searches yourself, so having someone else do the search for you saves some time. Sure, you have to do the filtering and dig through the results for any viable options, but Sales Navigator's algorithms have done the first part of the process for you.

You can spare a few minutes each day — I recommend you take just six minutes a day! — to take advantage of the work that Sales Navigator has already done for you, right?

Managing Your Sales Navigator Inbox

I get it. You have numerous email inboxes and it feels like you're never going to get down to the envied "Inbox Zero." (Does that even exist?) So why in the world would you want to add another inbox to an already overwhelming amount of email?

Well, luckily for you, I'm suggesting you spend only *six minutes a day* managing your Sales Navigator inbox. As a comparison, that's about how long it takes your neighborhood barista to brew up your favorite coffee drink in the morning. Well, I guess that depends on how complicated your drink order is, but still. It'll go by in a flash, I promise.

Your Sales Navigator inbox looks similar to the one you see in Figure 9-5. To access your Sales Navigator inbox, click the icon in the main navigation bar at the top of your screen that looks like two conversation bubbles. Figure 9-5 shows the default view, which consists of your existing messages in the left column, with unread messages sporting a little blue dot on the right side of the person's name.

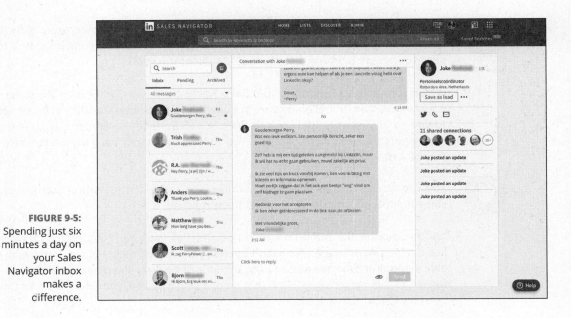

FIGURE 9-5: Spending just six minutes a day on your Sales Navigator inbox makes a difference.

At the top of the column of messages is a search box with three links underneath: Inbox, Pending, and Archived. As I mentioned, the inbox view is the default you'll always land on when you visit your inbox. The Archived view shows the messages you've moved from your inbox to save them. The middle link, Pending, is where the InMails you've sent — that haven't been opened yet — reside. Once a message that was in the Pending view is opened, it moves to the inbox view.

TIP

Keeping an eye on the Pending tab of your inbox is a good way to ensure you're staying within your monthly InMail allotment. As I discuss in Chapter 1, Sales Navigator Team-level accounts get 30 InMails per month, while Enterprise-level accounts get 50 InMails per month. It isn't possible to purchase additional InMail credits, so use yours wisely!

The largest section of your Sales Navigator inbox is the middle pane, where the text of the messages shows up when you click them. This is also where you reply to messages you've received. The entire record of your conversation with an individual is in this window, making it convenient to refer back to at any point.

All the way to the right side of the inbox screen is another column that displays information about the person whose conversation you are currently viewing in the center column. Here you can save this person as a lead (if he or she isn't one already), contact this person outside of LinkedIn (if he or she provided additional contact information), and see your shared connections and the general geographical area the person lives in. In other words, it's a little section of helpful information all in one place.

REMEMBER

When you have numerous conversations going at once, it's nice to be able to quickly know exactly who you're talking to, instead of having to click the link to view the person's profile directly to find this information.

Why is it important to manage your Sales Navigator inbox? There are a few different reasons. The first is obvious — you want to know when someone reaches out to you so you can respond back. It doesn't matter if it's a stranger, an existing lead, a potential lead, or a customer. You should always give each person the courtesy of a timely reply.

TIP

You can attach files to messages, so take advantage of this option and include some helpful informational material if appropriate.

Another reason it's important to stay on top of your Sales Navigator inbox is because you want to see who hasn't opened your InMail message yet. If a reasonable amount of time has passed (say, a couple of weeks), you may consider reaching out to this person again. Or if that's not a viable option, you know to strike this person off your list of leads.

A third reason managing your Sales Navigator inbox is important is because you can ensure you're following through with what you told someone you'd do. Whether it was to send additional information or reply back with someone else's contact information, skimming through your messages on a daily basis ensures nothing is falling through the cracks.

And last but certainly not least, you should sign into your Sales Navigator inbox every day because how else are you going to message people within the program? Whether it's InMail or an instant message to a person you're connected with, you should always be reaching out, even if it's just to touch base or congratulate someone on a job change. It helps you stay top of mind with your leads and existing customers, and it shows the rest of your network that you're paying attention to what's going on in their careers as well.

Engaging with Leads Using PointDrive

The remaining six minutes of my recommended 30-minute daily routine is centered around engaging with leads using Sales Navigator's PointDrive. PointDrive, which I discuss in Chapter 7, is a feature included with some Team-level Sales Navigator plans and all Enterprise-level plans that allows you to create, store, and manage presentations that are then packaged up to be sent to leads in a professional way. Prospects receive a personalized, branded content collection, instead of the usual email with multiple attachments.

Furthermore, content can be delivered at different points in the sales cycle, giving you even more insight into the buying process. All this data is collected and presented to you in easy-to-understand analytics so you can track your leads' engagement and adjust your strategy as needed.

To access PointDrive, hover your mouse pointer over the grid of six squares that appear in the main navigation menu bar at the top of your screen on and select PointDrive from the options that appear. The PointDrive presentations landing page appears, similar to the one shown in Figure 9-6. This default view shows all the presentations you've created with the newest on top.

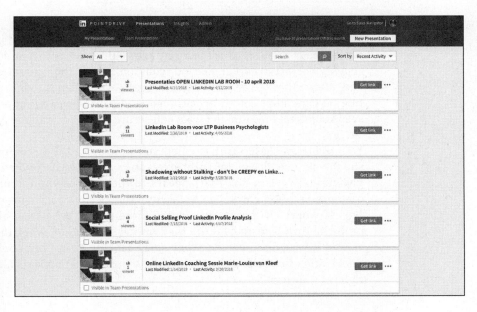

FIGURE 9-6: The PointDrive landing page is where all of my content is stored.

Each entry gives helpful information, such as the number of times your presentation has been viewed, when it was last viewed, and when it was last modified. You can also download a link to the presentation with the Get Link button. Clicking the three dots next to this button enables you to edit, view, and set different options for the presentation such as download prevention, password protection, and adding an expiration date, as shown in Figure 9-7.

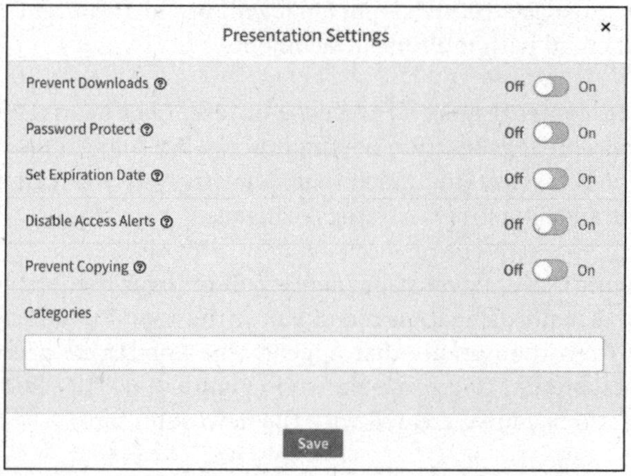

FIGURE 9-7:
Prevent
downloading and
set an expiration
date under the
settings menu.

I recommend you use some of these settings for a few reasons. First, you want to protect your intellectual property by preventing viewers from downloading and copying the presentation. Second, you don't want the content sticking around long after either the deal has gone through — or fallen through. That's why setting an expiration date is always a good idea. Finally, setting a password helps keep proprietary information safe and secure.

You decide on these settings when you first upload the presentation, so what should you be doing in PointDrive on a daily basis? When you click the <Number> Viewers link that appears to the right of the thumbnail picture in each presentation entry, you're taken to the Viewers page shown in Figure 9-8. This is where all the viewers of the presentation are listed, along with their profile blurbs, how many times they viewed the content, when the last time they viewed it was, and how long they spent looking at it. (You access this specific information by clicking the View Activity button that appears all the way to the right of the entry.)

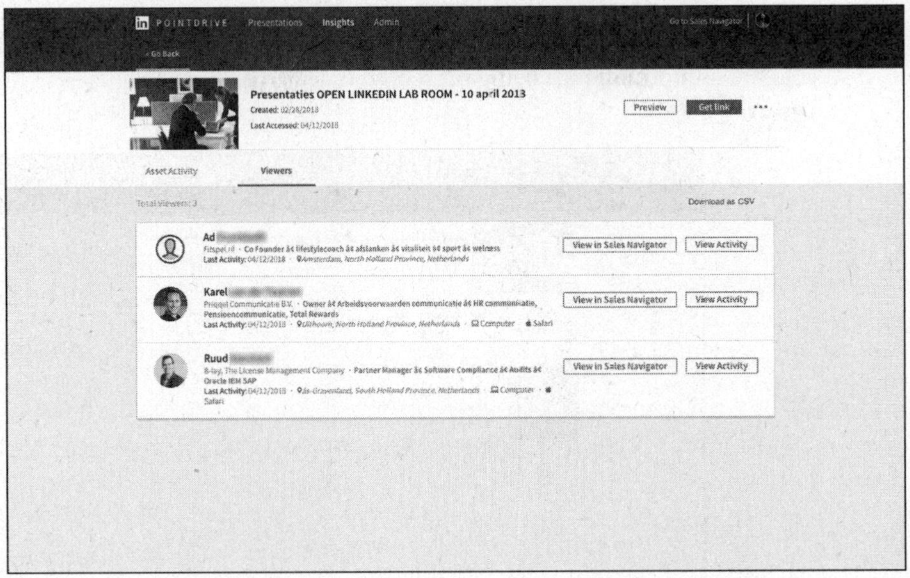

FIGURE 9-8:
Get the details on
who is viewing
your content.

By keeping an eye on who is viewing your presentations as well as the specific viewing details of each individual, you can see who the most interested parties are so you can follow up with them to keep the sales cycle alive. The worst thing you can do is hand out informational content and then wait for them to call! You have to take the bull by the horns, so to speak.

Another reason why it's a good idea to check out the Viewers page every day is to keep track of a lead's interest in your product or service. For example, a lead may have "gone dark" for a while and when you followed up, you were told the project had been shelved. But then you notice that the lead viewed your presentation again, this time spending even more time viewing it. This is a good indicator that the project may have been rejuvenated and it's time you reach out to the lead again to get top of mind.

Also on the Viewers page is a link underneath the presentation thumbnail picture for Asset Activity (see Figure 9-9). The Asset Activity page tells you how your content is performing overall. It offers insight into which presentations are getting opened and viewed the most and which aren't getting any interest at all. If something seems to be falling flat, it may be time to either refresh it with new, updated information, or retire it altogether.

REMEMBER

Staying on top of the health of your content ensures that only the highest quality information is being presented to leads.

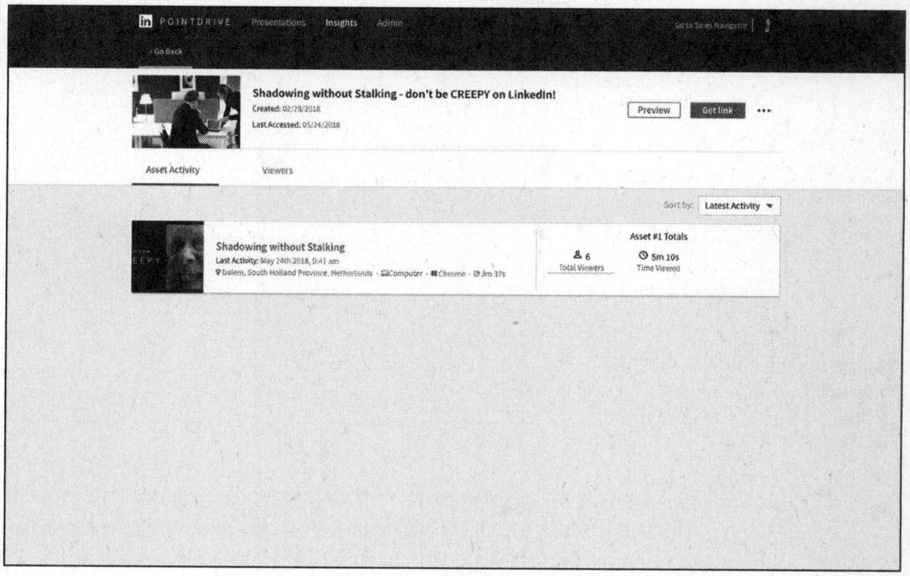

FIGURE 9-9:
The Asset Activity page shows you how your presentation is performing.

Chapter **10**

Using the Mobile App

S earching for sales prospects used to mean you were tied to your desktop computer or landline telephone. Today's technology enables us to take pretty much our entire lives with us on the go in our smartphones and tablets. Such is the case with the LinkedIn Sales Navigator mobile app. Meant to supplement the main desktop version of Sales Navigator, the mobile app lacks some of the same features of the desktop version, but that doesn't mean it's not incredibly handy and helpful . . . because it is!

In this chapter, I show you how to navigate the Sales Navigator mobile app home screen and I give you tips about what to keep an eye on while on the go. I also talk about how to find new leads via Sales Navigator's suggestions as well as via the search function. Finally, I take you through how to use the messaging feature as well as the importance of setting your sales preferences.

Accessing the Sales Navigator App

The Sales Navigator mobile app is available for both iOS and Android devices; however, for the purposes for this book, I am using an Apple iPhone for instructions and screenshots. Having said that, the apps for both platforms look and behave similarly, so you should have no trouble following along with your Android device.

To start, download the app from the main Sales Navigator Mobile app page (`https://business.linkedin.com/sales-solutions/sales-navigator/mobile-sales-app`), as shown in Figure 10-1. Another option is to download it from the applicable app store.

REMEMBER

You must have a Sales Navigator subscription to use the mobile app.

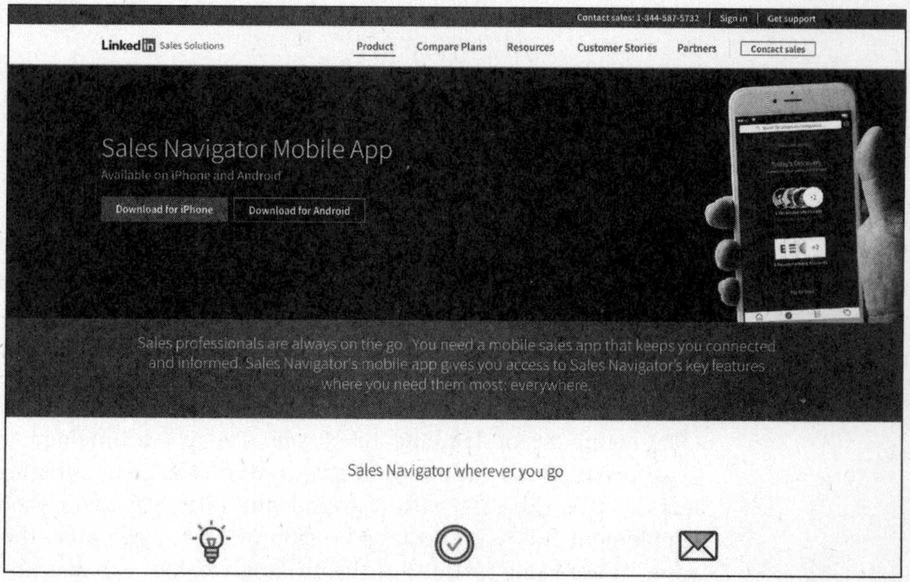

FIGURE 10-1:
Download Sales Navigator to your iOS or Android device from this page.

Once the app finishes downloading, launch the app by tapping the icon on your screen. Once it finishes loading, you see a login screen similar to the one shown in Figure 10-2. Enter your LinkedIn login information and tap the Sign In box. You then see your home screen, which will look similar to Figure 10-3.

REMEMBER

Even though you're in the Sales Navigator app (and not the actual LinkedIn app), you still use your LinkedIn login credentials.

Now that you're all logged in, we're ready to dive deeper into this helpful app!

FIGURE 10-2:
Here is where you log into your LinkedIn account.

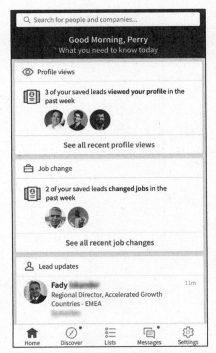

FIGURE 10-3:
The mobile app home screen is where you land once you log in.

Monitoring Activity on Your Home Screen

Just as with the desktop version of Sales Navigator, the home screen of the Sales Navigator mobile app is the central location from where you navigate throughout the app. Refer to Figure 10-3. Notice at the very top of the screen is the search bar where you can search for people and companies.

The section below that is called Profile Views, which is exactly what it sounds like — a list of people who have viewed your LinkedIn profile. The profile photos Sales Navigator displays in this section are those of any leads of yours who viewed your profile within the past week. What a quick and easy way to see right away who you should think about following up with! Below those photos is a link that says "See all recent profile views," which, when tapped, brings up a list of individuals who have viewed your profile in the past three weeks, as shown in Figure 10-4.

FIGURE 10-4: These people have viewed my profile within the past three weeks.

Beneath the profile blurb of each of these people is a button that says "Reach out." When you tap this button, Sales Navigator brings up an empty message box where you can compose and send a chat message to that individual.

Staying up to date on your leads' activities

Underneath the Profile Views section of the Sales Navigator mobile app home screen is a section that shows which people in your network have changed jobs in the past week. As was the case with profile views, the profile photos you see displayed in this section are those of saved leads who have recently changed jobs. To see the entire list, tap the "See all recent job changes" link at the bottom of that section. A list of every lead who has recently changed jobs is listed, along with a Reach Out button, as shown in Figure 10-5. Why don't you go ahead and send a note of congratulations?

REMEMBER

On the desktop app, the time frame for showing job changes is within the past 90 days.

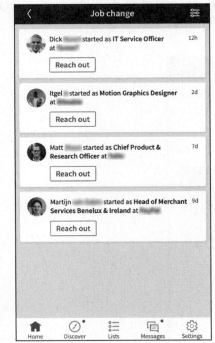

FIGURE 10-5:
People who have changed jobs in the past week.

TIP

Congratulating someone on a job change (or other achievement) is a great way to become top of mind, even if the person isn't a prospect at the moment. Everyone likes to be recognized.

Beneath the Job Change section of the mobile app home screen is the Lead Updates section. Only one entry is shown in this section at a time. To view more lead updates from your other leads, tap the "View more lead updates" link at the bottom of that section to expand the screen. The Leads Updates screen can be sorted by News updates, which consist of work anniversaries (with the option to reach out to these leads to offer congratulations, of course) and lead Shares, which consist of updates from your leads that contain things like links to outside articles or general text status updates.

The last section on the home screen is Account Updates. Just as with the Lead Updates section, only one update is displayed on the screen, but tapping the "View more account updates" link at the bottom expands the section to show more. The default view on the Account Updates screen is Shares, which displays the content a company's LinkedIn business page posts. You are also given the option to "Like" the post (see Figure 10-6). Tapping the News heading brings up a screen that shows any news articles recently published about the accounts you have saved. To see the entire article, tap the View link.

FIGURE 10-6:
Don't forget to
tap "Like!"

Filtering your updates

At the bottom of the mobile app home screen is a link that says "Filter your updates." Tapping that link pulls up the menu shown in Figure 10-7, which enables you to filter your leads' activities based on profile views, job changes, lead updates, account updates, or all insights (which takes you back to the main home screen).

TIP

You can access this filter menu from any detailed updates screen by tapping the icon in the top right of the screen that looks like three dots and three lines.

Filtering your updates by one of these headings is a great way to quickly narrow down the specific type of update you're looking for. For example, if you're just looking for people who have viewed your profile in the past week, simply tap the Profile Views option in this menu and your home page results are sorted to only show those who have recently checked out your LinkedIn profile.

TIP

Make a mistake or want to get back to the original view? Tap the All Insights option in this menu to list each lead activity section as listed on the mobile app home screen.

Filter your updates

Profile views

Lead updates

Account updates

All Insights

Cancel

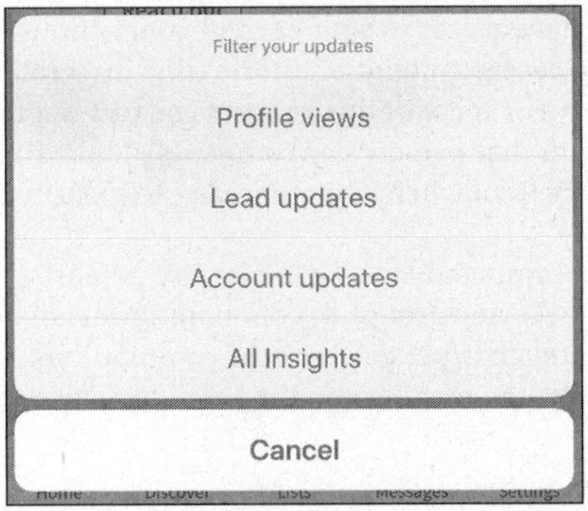

FIGURE 10-7: Filtering your updates.

Engaging with your leads

In Chapters 1 and 7, I discuss the importance of making connections and building a rapport with people in order to build up a network of leads who will (hopefully) facilitate sales in the future. When people like you, they're most likely to trust — and buy — from you. While Sales Navigator is a great tool to facilitate this connection-making, it doesn't do all the heavy lifting for you. In other words, you have to engage! You have to make sure you're interacting with leads so that you get on their radars.

Engaging can mean a couple of things. You can use one of the provided buttons to "like" or otherwise show your appreciation for a lead's or account's content. You can share a lead's content using one of the network's methods or you can take the time to write a comment. The desktop version of Sales Navigator has a couple more options to engage; however, the mobile app still gives you the chance to do so.

TIP

The more time you invest in engaging with leads, the better your chances for catching their attention. In other words, taking the time to write a thoughtful comment on a post holds more weight than clicking the thumbs up button.

Identifying potential new leads

As I mention earlier in this chapter, the Sales Navigator mobile app lacks some of the functionality of the desktop version. Because of this, I don't recommend you use it as your primary method of accessing Sales Navigator. One of the ways the mobile app is much less robust is with the search feature. While searching with the mobile app is sufficient, it's not as detailed and as powerful as the search feature in the desktop version of Sales Navigator.

All is not lost, however. You can still identify new leads using the mobile app. You already know that you have access to your current connections and their LinkedIn profiles. You can gain a decent amount of information by scrolling through a person's profile on the app. For most of the sections you can tap the specific account or profile and be taken to that person's or company's LinkedIn profile page. This capability is extremely helpful when you're looking to identify new leads.

WARNING

One of the top ways I recommend looking to identify potential new leads is to see if you and that person have any groups in common. Unfortunately, while you can see what groups you and that person have in common, you cannot access the group's LinkedIn page on the mobile app; therefore, you're unable to prospect in that way on the app.

When you're looking for prospective leads, pull up the LinkedIn profile of one of your existing connections and scroll down to the People Also Viewed section. (It's usually at the bottom of the profile.) Most of these people are probably second-degree connections to you — close enough of a connection that one of your first-degree connections may be willing to give you a warm introduction. If your first-degree connection is a member of your TeamLink, all the better! (See Chapter 5 for more about using TeamLink to prospect for potential leads.)

Once you locate a person of interest in the People Also Viewed section of your connection's profile, tap that person's profile blurb to see all of his or her information. If you think the person is a potential lead, tap the Save as Lead button. This person's profile is added to your leads list and you are subscribed to his or her updates. Depending on the person's settings, there may also be a button to send an InMail message. Since you only get a certain number of InMails per month, I recommend only sending one if you're really confident this person is open to communicating with you. You may want to wait a while to become more acquainted with this person by keeping an eye on what types of updates he or she posts.

Perusing Recommendations in Today's Discovery

One helpful feature of the Sales Navigator mobile app is the Today's Discovery section. To open the Today's Discovery screen, tap the Discover icon (it looks like a compass) that is located at the bottom of your mobile app home screen. A screen like the one shown in Figure 10-8 appears, which shows you recommended leads and accounts based on the sales preferences you selected when you first set up your Sales Navigator account.

WARNING

These recommendations are only around for 15 hours (literally, there's a countdown), so you have to act fact if you want to check them all out!

To view these suggestions, either tap within the applicable section (the top group lists recommended leads and the bottom group lists recommended accounts) or tap the Tap to Start link at the bottom of the page. Either action brings you to your first recommendation.

Once you're on that person's profile page, you can choose to dismiss him or her as a lead by tapping the Dismiss button or save this person as a lead by tapping the Save button. If you're unsure and want to learn more about the person first, tap the "View more" link at the bottom of the screen to expand the profile. Easy, right?

TIP

To toggle between the Recommend Leads and Recommended Accounts screens, tap the corresponding heading at the top of your screen, which brings up the screen you see in Figure 10-9. On that screen you can select which section you want to view. Once you decide how you want to handle a lead or account, simply swipe your finger to the right on the screen to bring up the next recommendation and repeat the process.

FIGURE 10-8:
The Today's Discovery landing page.

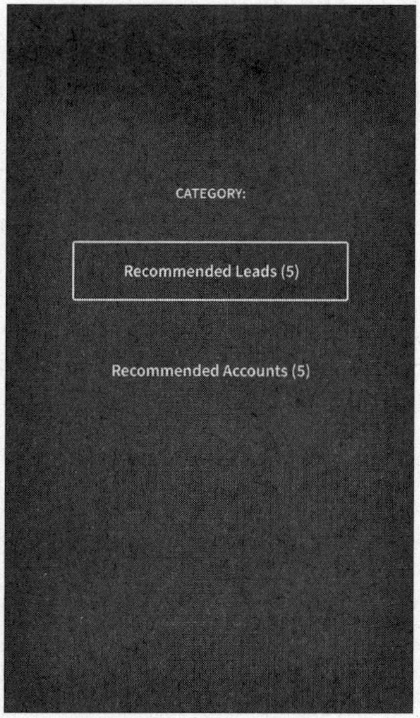

CATEGORY:

Recommended Leads (5)

Recommended Accounts (5)

FIGURE 10-9:
Easily switch between viewing leads and accounts.

Sales Navigator presents ten potential leads and accounts to follow per day — five suggested leads and five suggested accounts. In the top-right corner of the screen is a number that keeps track of how many recommendations you have remaining to view. For example, if you've swiped once and see "2/10" in the top-right corner, you know you're looking at the second suggestion. Figure 10-10 shows you what a recommended account screen looks like.

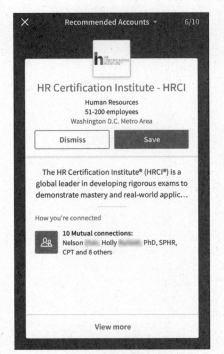

FIGURE 10-10:
LinkedIn recommends I save this account.

Searching with the Sales Navigator App

The search function in the Sales Navigator mobile app is not nearly as robust as it is in the desktop version. In fact, it offers fewer sorting and filtering options than even the basic search in the desktop version. We can't really hold that against LinkedIn, though. There's only so much functionality an app can have before it becomes a muddled mess. After all, the app is meant to be a supplemental option, not the main way to access Sales Navigator.

However, the mobile app *does* have search capabilities that can be quite helpful on the fly. When you tap the search bar at the top of your mobile home screen, you see a screen that looks like Figure 10-11. You can type in a specific person's or company's name or a keyword or words to pull up companies and individuals with those words in their names or headlines. For example, if you search for the phrase *web hosting*, the search returns results of companies with "web hosting" in its name or people who included that phrase in their profiles' headlines.

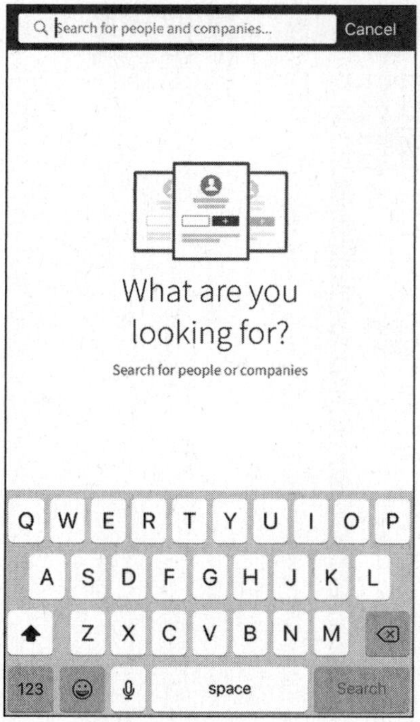

FIGURE 10-11: Sales Navigator is ready for your search request.

Using Boolean operators

Boolean operators are two (or more) words used in searches that instruct the app's search capabilities to take into consideration words entered in a certain way. The most common words used in Boolean searches are "AND," "OR," and "NOT." For example, I want to search for leads and accounts that contain the words *social* and *selling*. My results are shown in Figure 10-12.

Employing keywords when performing searches helps narrow down search results so that you don't have to go through the results one by one and strip away any that aren't exactly what you're looking for. Think of the time and energy you save! For more about using Boolean operators in searches, see Chapter 5.

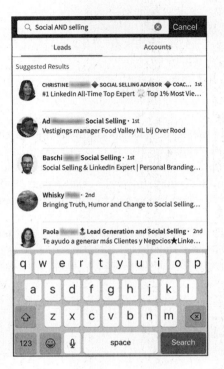

FIGURE 10-12:
I used the
Boolean operator
"AND" to search
for *social* and
selling.

Filtering leads with Sales Spotlights

As I discuss in Chapter 5, Sales Spotlights is a Sales Navigator feature that uses LinkedIn's data to select the prospects who are most likely to be receptive to a message from you. Sales Spotlights are only available on search results pages. Clicking within each section highlights the section in blue, indicating that the results you see reflect that specific Sales Spotlight.

The mobile app includes the same Sales Spotlight categories you'll find in the desktop version of Sales Navigator. However, you have a lot less functionality when it comes to the information you're presented with or the actions you can take directly in the app.

In addition to the total search results, Sales Spotlights for leads are broken down into six different categories:

>> Changed jobs in the past 90 days

>> Leads with TeamLink intro

>> Mentioned in the news in the past 30 days

>> Posted on LinkedIn in the past 30 days

>> Share experiences with you

>> Leads that follow your company on LinkedIn

Total results

The first section you see in the list of Sales Spotlights is the search's Total Results. This filter lists all of your search results that aren't segmented down into the different Sales Spotlight options. Total Results always shows the highest number of results and is the default view on your search results page. See Figure 10-13 for the search results I received when I searched for the phrase *social selling*.

TIP

Tapping the plus sign (+) next to a person's name saves that person to your list as a lead. When you add a person to your list like this, the plus sign changes to the word *Saved*. Tapping the word *Saved* unsaves the lead. This applies to all Sales Spotlight sections.

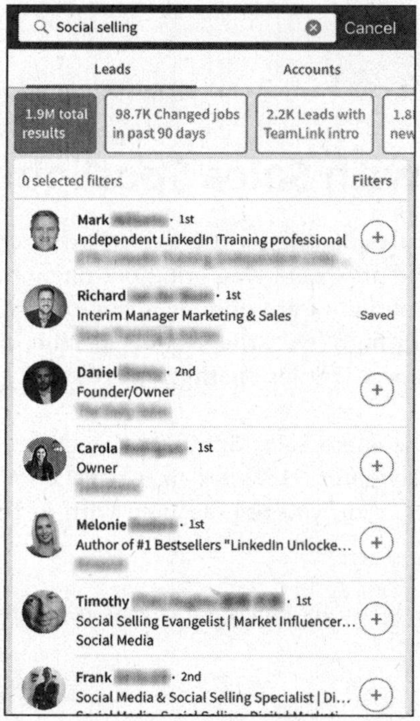

FIGURE 10-13:
The total results of this search is 1.9 million.

Changed jobs

The first Sales Spotlight section that appears to the right of Total Results is "Changed jobs in the past 90 days," which displays the number of leads in this search results list that have recently made a career change in the past 90 days. Unlike in the desktop version of Sales Navigator, however, the search results don't show any specific job change details.

TIP

If you want to know the person's previous position, tap his or her entry in this list and scroll down to the Experience section to look at his or her employment dates.

Knowing that someone has changed jobs is helpful for a few reasons. First is the fact that this change may have made this person a closer connection to you, whether it's through your general LinkedIn network or your colleagues and TeamLink. It just may mean a warmer introduction for you. This information also gives you a reason to reach out. It's common for people on LinkedIn to congratulate others on new positions. While you may not know the lead personally, a job change is a legitimate reason for reaching out.

TeamLink leads

TeamLink leads are unique in that you have built-in warm introductions to prospects because they are connected to your team members. Tapping a person's profile blurb brings up the person's full profile where you can send him or her a message or, if he or she isn't already a lead, save him or her as a lead. I discuss TeamLink in more detail in Chapters 1 and 5.

Mentioned in the news

Another great way to break the ice with someone is by mentioning something he or she has done that was recently published in the news. This is why Sales Navigator created a spotlight specifically for it.

Being mentioned in the news is a perfect reason to reach out to a prospect. After all, who doesn't like to be written up in the news (for a positive reason, at least) and for your professional network to have seen it? When reaching out to a potential lead, tell the prospect that you saw the piece and add in an anecdote or two related to the subject matter to let him or her know that you paid attention and actually care.

Posted on LinkedIn

Not everyone who has a LinkedIn profile is active on the social network. People may have forgotten that they signed up or maybe they decided it wasn't useful for them. Whatever the reason, it's a waste of time for social-selling professionals to try to connect with people who will never see their messages. That's where the "Posted on LinkedIn in the past 30 days" Sales Spotlight filter comes into play.

Now you can see who has logged into their LinkedIn accounts in the last month. This makes it easy for you to decide whether or not you want to take the chance that a prospect won't see a message you send because he or she is not an active user of LinkedIn.

Shared experiences

In Chapter 8, I talk about different ways to connect with leads, and the "Share experiences with you" Sales Spotlight filter is the perfect place to start collecting those ideas (see Figure 10-14). After filtering your search results with the "Share experiences with you" Sales Spotlight, tap any one of the profile blurbs to bring up that person's full profile where you can see your shared experiences underneath the Highlights section. Being able to refer to a group you both belong to, for example, is a helpful way to break the ice.

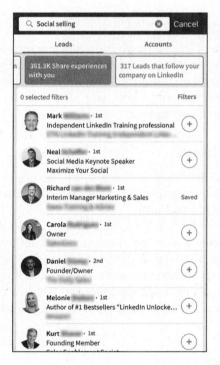

FIGURE 10-14: Filter your search results with the "Share experiences with you" Sales Spotlight to see who shares experiences with you.

Leads that follow your company

The final Sales Spotlight for leads is the "Leads that follow your company on LinkedIn" filter. This filter shows the leads who follow your company page on LinkedIn. That means you and/or your company are on the radar of the leads in these results. How's that for a foot in the door?

But how do you leverage this information? Reach out to these connections. Mention that you see they're following your company page and ask whether they have any questions about the products or services your company offers. Knowing that the lead is already aware of your company is a great sign and it's one you should take advantage of!

Filtering accounts with Sales Spotlights

Sales Spotlights for accounts are broken down into two different sections: total results and accounts that had senior leadership changes in the last three months.

Total results

Total Results is the same as the Total Results of a leads search. This filter lists all your search results that aren't segmented down into the different Sales Spotlight options. This filter always shows the highest number of results and is the default view on your search results page.

Senior leadership changes

The "Senior leadership changes in the last 3 months" Sales Spotlight lists all of those companies who have had changes in senior leadership within the past 90 days. See Figure 10-15 for the search results for the phrase *social selling*. This could be valuable information for you because maybe you were nurturing a lead for a couple of months and all of a sudden that person is no longer there and your phone calls and email messages are going unanswered. Now you know why.

Applying additional filters

The Sales Spotlights aren't the only filters available to help you narrow down your search results so that you can hone in on the most promising prospects. On the search results screen underneath the Sales Spotlight filters is the word *Filters* (see Figure 10-16). Tapping that brings up the screen shown in Figure 10-17.

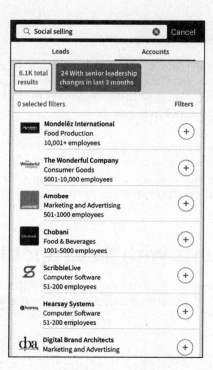

FIGURE 10-15:
These companies had changes in the upper echelon in the past 90 days.

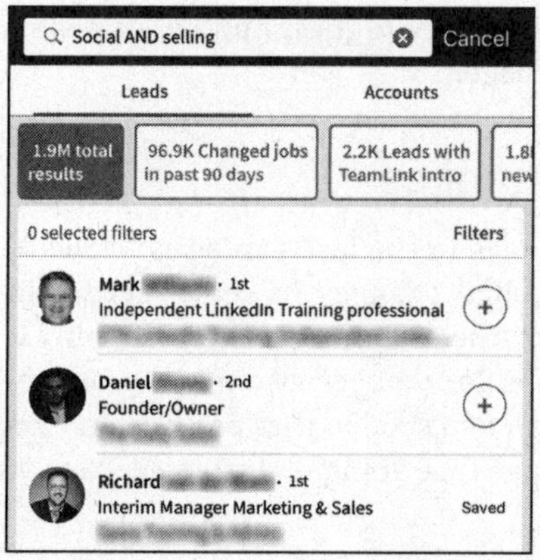

FIGURE 10-16:
Tap the word *Filters* to see more filtering options.

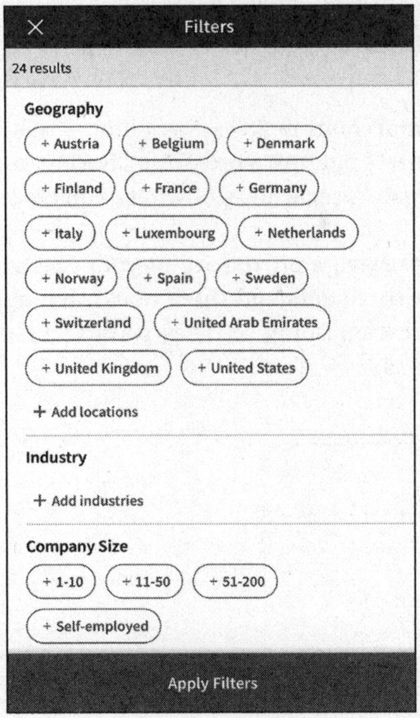

FIGURE 10-17:
You can apply
even more filters
to narrow down
your search
results.

While there are considerably fewer filtering options than in the desktop version of Sales Navigator, the mobile app offers the most important and useful filters when looking to narrow down your search results. These filters are:

>> Exclude Saved Leads

>> Search Within Saved Accounts

>> Geography

>> Relationship

>> Industry

>> Company Size

>> Function

>> Title

>> Seniority Level

You can add a filter by tapping the "+ Add" links at the bottom of each section. To remove a filter, tap the specific selection you want to remove and then tap the "X" that appears to the left of the filter name.

Managing Saved Leads

Whenever you save a lead or account in Sales Navigator — whether in the mobile app or desktop version — it gets put into a list. Your saved lists are accessible from either version of Sales Navigator, regardless of where you created it.

In the mobile version of Sales Navigator, you access your saved lists by tapping the Lists icon (it's the one with three dots and three lines) that appears in the menu bar on the bottom of your screen. Doing so takes you to a Lists screen similar to the one shown in Figure 10-18.

FIGURE 10-18: The Leads tab of the Lists screen.

Tap to open saved lists

Adding and editing tags and notes

Sales Navigator lets you add tags and notes to your saved leads to help you keep your account organized. *Tags* put leads into groups that can help you find what you need fast. *Notes* are ways to store information about leads, such as the last time you touched base with them or the types of content they respond best to.

To add tags to a lead, follow these steps:

1. **From the lead's LinkedIn profile page, tap the "+ Add new tag" link in the center of the screen.**

   If you've created tags before, those tags appear on the next screen with check marks next to them (see Figure 10-19). If you have not created any tags before, you only see the six tags Sales Navigator provides: Customer, Decision Maker, Follow Up, High Priority, Influencer, and Opportunity. For more information on tags, see Chapter 6.

2. **Select all applicable tags or create new tags by typing the desired word into the empty box at the top and tapping the plus sign (+) that appears.**

3. **If you decide you want to edit or delete tags from your existing list, tap the name of the tag and then tap the circled check mark to uncheck it.**

   If you decide you want to remove other tags as well, you can do it at this time.

4. **When you are finished adding tags, tap Save that appears at the top-right of the screen.**

   You are taken back to the lead's profile page.

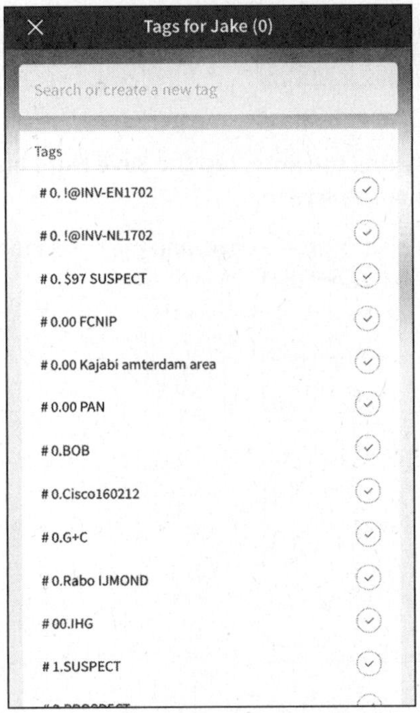

FIGURE 10-19: Select tags from the existing list or create a new tag.

To add and edit notes on a lead's profile, follow these steps:

1. **From the lead's LinkedIn profile page, tap the "+ Add new note" link in the center of the screen.**

   A blank screen appears where you can start typing your note, as shown in Figure 10-20. You have enough space for 512 characters.

FIGURE 10-20:
Add a new note
here.

2. **When you're finished typing the note, tap the Save Note button that appears at the bottom of the screen.**

   You are taken back to the lead's profile page, and the note appears under the notes section, as shown in Figure 10-21.

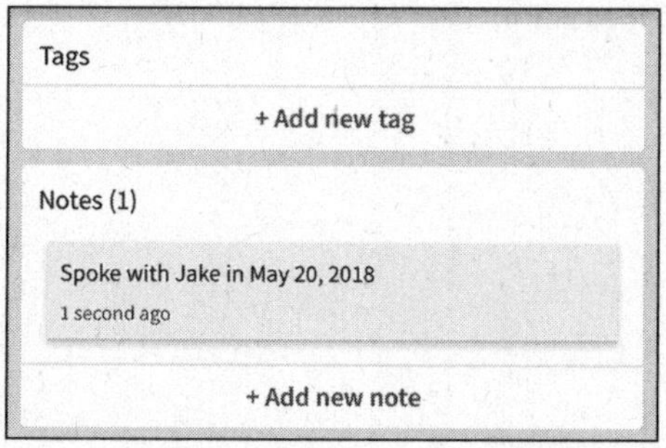

FIGURE 10-21:
An existing note
on a profile page.

3. **To edit a note, tap the note on a lead's profile page.**

   You are taken to the note's home page.

4. **Tap the pencil icon that appears on the right side of the note to bring up the editing screen.**

   Tap the Save Note button when you are finished editing to return to the lead's profile page.

Sending and checking messages

Another helpful feature of the Sales Navigator mobile app is the capability to send and receive LinkedIn messages directly within the app. While typing lengthy messages on a mobile device isn't the most convenient method of communication, it's available in case a lead has a time-sensitive question, for example.

To access your LinkedIn messages, tap the Messages icon that appears in the menu bar on the bottom of your screen. When on the Messages screen, you can search for a person or message by typing that person's name or a keyword into the search box at the top of the screen. You can also filter your messages by Pending, Archived, Sent, and Unread by tapping the icon that looks like three dots and three lines in the top-right portion of the Messages screen (Figure 10-22). If you want to compose a message, tap the pencil and paper icon that appears above the filter icon in the top right of the screen.

TIP

You can also send a message directly from the person's profile.

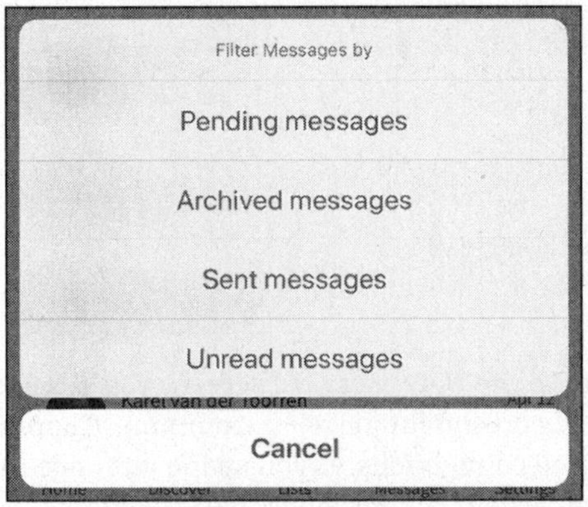

FIGURE 10-22:
Filter your
messages.

Filter Messages by

Pending messages

Archived messages

Sent messages

Unread messages

Karel van der Toorren

Cancel

Once you're on the New Message screen, either search for the person you want to message by typing that person's name in the search bar at the top (if you didn't initiate the message from that person's profile) or just start typing your message in the big empty box on your screen.

You'll notice three small icons at the bottom of the message box: a photo, a camera, and a lightbulb. The first two icons may be familiar to you. They let you attach a picture or take a picture to attach to the message. The third icon may be a little different from what you've seen before, however. Tapping the lightbulb icon brings up the current employment information of the person to whom you're writing, as shown in Figure 10-23. This could be helpful if, for example, you need something to spur your memory about a past conversation you had with the recipient.

Tap to show information
about the recipient

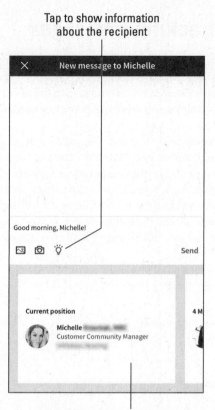

FIGURE 10-23:
Tap the lightbulb
icon to show
more information
about the
message
recipient.

Swipe left to discover more you have
in common with this contact

TIP

If you swipe to the left in the New Message screen, you'll see a box showing the connections you and the recipient have in common. Tapping inside this box expands the list of shared connections. If you swipe left once more, you'll see any LinkedIn Groups you and the recipient may have in common. Using the information in these boxes is a great way to break the ice with a prospect.

Accessing Your Account Settings

While the Sales Navigator mobile app lacks a lot of the functionality of the desktop version, you can customize a few settings to personalize your mobile Sales Navigator experience.

REMEMBER

Changing settings on the mobile app does not affect your settings on the desktop app and vice versa.

Selecting your sales preferences

To access the mobile app settings, tap the gear icon that appears in the menu bar on the bottom of your screen. The Sales Preferences screen appears. On the Sales Preferences screen under the settings menu you can set your preferred geographical area, industry, company size, and function. These selections help LinkedIn provide you with more relevant lead and account suggestions.

To add sales preferences, simply tap the plus sign (+) to the right of the setting you want to add. On the next screen that appears, either search for the option you want or scroll down until you find it. Once you locate it, tap to select it (the circle with the check mark turns blue). If you want to deselect an option, simply tap the circle again. When you're finished adding (or deleting) preferences, tap the left-pointing arrow that appears in the top-left corner of the screen to return to the Sales Preferences screen.

Determining your settings

Tapping the word *Settings* that appears to the right of the Sales Preferences tab at the top of the Settings screen opens the general settings tab shown in Figure 10-24. Along with toggling push notifications on or off (allowing Sales Navigator to alert you to activity by your saved leads and accounts), sending feedback, and viewing the privacy and security policies, you should pay attention to two important options on this tab: Your Social Selling Index and Calendar Sync Settings.

Viewing your Social Selling Index

I discuss the Social Selling Index (SSI) in detail in Chapter 1, but as a quick reminder, your SSI a gauge of how well your social-selling activities on Sales Navigator are performing that day. It measures how effective you are at establishing your personal brand, finding the right leads, engaging with purpose, and building relationships.

You access this information by tapping the "Your Social Selling Index" link on the Settings tab. It is the first option under the Account heading. Here you can see not only your SSI, but also how you rank in your industry and network.

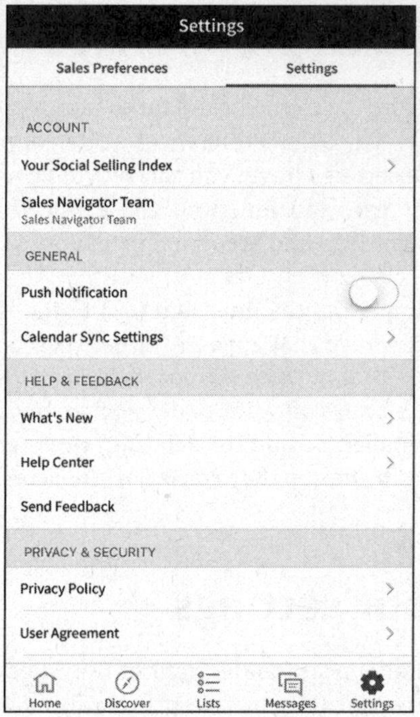

FIGURE 10-24:
The Settings tab.

Syncing your calendar

The second setting I want to call your attention to is the "Calendar Sync Settings" link under the General heading. This setting offers the ability to sync your calendar to your Sales Navigator mobile account. Syncing your calendar is helpful because you can get reminders about events in once place, without having to set reminders in multiple apps. That way, when you're on the road attending sales meetings, you don't have to worry that you're missing other important appointments. To enable this setting, simply tap the toggle button and approve Sales Navigator's access to your calendar by tapping the Settings button in the box that pops up and tapping the Calendars toggle on the following screen.

5
The Part of Tens

Chapter **11**

Ten Tips for Advanced Lead Generation

You've made it through (pretty much) to the end of the book so you're a master at social selling with LinkedIn Sales Navigator, right? Of course, you are! Now that you've got the basics under your belt, I put together what I think are ten advanced lead-generation tips to help you take your social selling to the next level.

Quantity versus Quality

We all begin our sales careers with the same immediate goal: More! More! More! More contacts! More cold calls! More email addresses and phone numbers!

It's the same with Sales Navigator. When you first log in, Sales Navigator presents you with a number of suggested accounts to follow, and you can save as many as you'd like. While this is a good way to build up your initial contact list, it's not a sustainable methodology. After all, social selling is all about engaging with prospects. It's about getting to know them and their wants, needs, and pain points. It's about the one-on-one interactions with them that leaves them feeling that you actually care about helping, as opposed to just earning a commission.

That's why I'll always recommend that social-selling professionals choose *quality* leads and interactions over quantity. If you're doing your job, your sales numbers will grow organically. Take care of the few customers you have and you'll never have to network again, because those customers will be glad to recommend you to other people in their networks.

Saving Connections as Leads

While I'm a proponent of quality over quantity, that doesn't mean you shouldn't take advantage of your existing network and connections on LinkedIn. In fact, I highly recommend it! Your LinkedIn connections are individuals who are already familiar with you and your business. Chances are, you don't have to win them over. If you're presenting yourself and your business in a professional and engaging manner, you've already overcome one of the main (and major) hurdles of sales: gaining the customer's trust.

So, go ahead and import your connections from LinkedIn into your Sales Navigator account. Luckily, the program makes this easy for you. Just follow these steps:

1. **From your Sales Navigator home page, hover your mouse pointer over the Lists link in the main navigation menu bar at the top of your screen and select My Network from the drop-down menu.**

    You're taken to the My Network home page as shown in Figure 11-1. This page lists your first-, second-, and third-degree connections ("and everyone else"), as well as members of the Groups you belong to. Basically, your entire social network.

2. **Scroll down to the Relationships section in the filtering box on the left side of the screen and click the 1st Connections link.**

    This filters out all LinkedIn members except for those you are direct (first-degree) connections with.

3. **Apply any other filters you feel are appropriate.**

    For example, you may want to isolate those connections who work for a certain company, or only those who are in the C-suite.

4. **Scroll through your results and click the Save as Lead button for any connections you want to follow in Sales Navigator.**

    Once you save them, you have the option to reach out directly by messaging them to get the conversation started!

FIGURE 11-1:
The My Network
home page.

TIP

It's good practice to follow the accounts of your own business as well as those of competitors. The same thing goes for making leads of employees of said competitors and colleagues. It doesn't hurt to keep an ear to the ground to stay up to date on what's going on in your professional world.

Increasing Response Rates and Engagement with Your Profile

LinkedIn is a social network, first and foremost. Sure, it's a professional networking one, but it's still one built on the foundation of making social connections. That being said, the best way to increase response rates and engagement with your profile is by — yep, you guessed it — responding and engaging with other users. You can do this by giving their updates a thumbs up and, even better, leaving genuine comments and/or questions based on something they posted.

The keyword there is *genuine.* Make sure the comment is detailed and pertinent to the update. Don't just leave a generic comment such as, "Great post!" Sure, you're commenting, but it's almost better that you didn't because it comes across as impersonal and canned. A better comment would be, "Thanks for this post, Dave. It's very timely as I've just encountered this issue in my own company. It gave me a lot of insight." It's comments such as that that will catch Dave's attention and prompt him to respond in some way (if he, too, practices good social-networking etiquette). Once the ice is broken, Dave is more likely to be open to interacting with you in the future, including following and commenting on your updates. Social selling is very much quid pro quo.

REMEMBER

Do *not* start selling to connections the minute they acknowledge you or one of your posts. It's pretty much a guarantee you'll turn them off and they'll run for the hills.

Best Practices for Requesting an Introduction

Social networking in general is about making connections. While the other popular social networks are for personal use, LinkedIn is used to make professional connections.

It's not unheard of for people to request introductions to people in their extended network. In fact, it's expected. So much, in fact, that Sales Navigator has a built-in tool that facilitates the connecting of people through co-workers and colleagues — TeamLink. (TeamLink is discussed in detail in Chapter 5.)

For the purposes of this Part of Tens chapter, however, I'll list some best practices for requesting introductions that I've picked up over the course of my career:

>> **Make sure you know the person you're requesting an introduction from personally.** There's nothing worse than getting hit up for an introduction to a colleague by some guy you spoke with briefly at a conference a year ago. He's asking you to vouch for him to your colleague. There's a lot on the line for the person making the introduction. Don't put anyone in an awkward position by requesting an introduction from someone you barely know.

>> **For best results, ask for an introduction from someone you know who is in a more senior position.** When someone in a higher position professionally than you facilitates an introduction, it looks good for your level of professionalism as well as your quality of work. If this more senior person trusts you, chances are you're a trustworthy person, and that is a great message you want communicated.

>> **Try to find a common ground with the person you're requesting an introduction to and share that with the connector.** Sure, your connection can talk you up professionally, but to be able to point out that you both went to the same university (at the same time!) is worth its weight in gold. It could be any similarities: you belong to the same LinkedIn Groups or professional associations, or even something like you both worked at small telecommunications companies at one point in your careers.

>> **Don't ask the same person for introductions.** Sure, this person may know *a lot* of people and may be very well-respected in the industry, but if you're constantly hitting this connection up for introductions, he or she is going to start thinking that it's the only reason you wanted to connect in the first place.

>> **Create a template for the connector to use.** Make it clear that your connection doesn't have to use the template, of course, but chances are he or she will appreciate that you took a lot of the effort out of writing up the message. Your connection may also be grateful that you were able to really personalize the message with details about yourself that the connector may not know. It makes the introduction seem more genuine.

>> **Make it easy for the potential connector to decline.** No one wants to be turned down, of course. And it's just as awkward for the person doing the turning down. Let your connection know that regardless of whether he or she is able to fulfill your request, you are grateful that he or she took time to consider it.

Conversation Starters

You'll be hard-pressed to find a sales professional who actually enjoys cold-calling. (If you happen to be one of those unicorns, please share your secrets for loving it!) In Chapter 8, I discuss the importance of finding common ground with customers as people generally want to buy from people they like. Having some fodder to start a conversation can help you find this commonality and build a rapport more quickly.

Legend has it that if you have something of substance to talk about with a potential customer, that customer will be much more open to speaking with you, which can open even more doors to building a rapport with them. So, what are some safe and effective conversation starters? Here are a few:

>> **"What's keeping you busy lately?"** This is a great one because it opens up the possibility to get both personal and professional information about the

person. A variation of this (if it's directly on LinkedIn) is, "I've noticed that quite a few of your updates lately have been about <fill in the blank.> This seems like something you're passionate about. Where did this interest begin?"

>> **"I noticed that you're <writing about, listening to> podcasts, what are some of your favorites?"** Like with the previous suggestion, this lets the person know you've taken the time to notice an interest and care enough to ask about it. When a customer realizes you do truly care, the customer is more likely to trust you when you say that you can help solve a problem he or she may be having.

>> **"What's something in your industry you consider underrated?"** Many of us have discovered a helpful or engaging tool or an event speaker that others haven't taken notice of yet. Try to find out if this person has made such a discovery as well. In addition to learning about your prospect, you'll also learn some valuable information about the prospect's industry.

TIP

Tailor your conversation starters to where you're having the conversation. For example, having a conversation over InMail messages lends itself to different starters than conversations held face to face at an industry conference or social event.

Managing Your Sales Navigator Inbox

Once you build your network and leads list, your Sales Navigator InMail inbox is likely to get quite full. And the fact that it's probably one of a number of email inboxes that is demanding your attention just adds to the chance that a message may fall by the wayside. There's nothing worse than missing out on a lead because your Sales Navigator inbox hasn't been kept organized.

Here are some tips to help you manage your InMail messages:

>> **Archive messages you've read and acted upon.** There is no use in keeping them in your inbox if there's nothing left to do with them.

>> **Mark as "unread" messages you've opened but still have to reply to or otherwise act upon.** Keeping them unread will remind you that they need to be revisited.

>> **Keep an eye on the Pending tab.** The center tab of your inbox is for InMails that have yet to receive a response. Be sure to "keep tabs" (see what I did there?) on potential leads that you have reached out to so you can follow up in the future if appropriate.

>> **If an InMail message receives a response and is thereby moved to your main inbox, take advantage of the Save as Lead button on the right side of the page.** A conversation has started! Don't forget to nurture the lead and keep it going.

>> **Use the search box.** You're a busy sales professional, and between your inbox, sent, pending, and archived messages, there are a lot of communications floating around. Use the search box at the top of the inbox to make quick work of finding the message or messages you need.

InMail Do's and Don'ts

InMail messages can be an invaluable sales tool provided you don't abuse the privilege of being able to send messages to anyone on LinkedIn, regardless of your degree of connection. Here are a few do's and don'ts to ensure that you're InMail-ing at the top of your game:

>> **DO** research the recipient well to find common ground, such as similar groups, shared connections, or shared alma maters.

>> **DO** grab the recipient's attention with an eye-catching subject line. Make the person want to open up your message, but be careful not to sound, too spammy.

>> **DO** keep it brief. No one is going to read a wordy message from a stranger. Keep it short, sweet, and to the point. Consider bullet points or at least paragraph breaks to make the text easier to consume.

>> **DON'T** hound the recipient if he or she doesn't respond. Best-case scenario is that people get busy and things fall through the cracks. The worst-case scenario is that they're just not interested. Think carefully about reaching out again.

>> **DON'T** try to sell them something. Make this message about them, not about you and how great your product or service is.

>> **DO** include a call to action. Let the recipient know the next steps, whether it is downloading a tip sheet you're offering or even offering a connection request. Don't leave dead air.

Adding and Saving Your Default Signature

Another great feature of InMail is the ability to add a default signature to it, just like you can do in your regular email client. This ensures that your name, title, and other contact information is front and center in the InMail message, omitting the need for the message recipient to check out your profile in order to get in touch.

REMEMBER

While you want to make sure you have enough information in your email signature so that the message recipient can contact you, you want to be careful that you don't add information just to use up every one of the 150 characters you are allotted. Make sure what you're including is relevant.

To set your signature in InMail, follow these steps:

1. **From your Sales Navigator home page, click the inbox icon in the main navigation menu bar at the top of your screen.**

   Your inbox home page opens. The default view is of your unarchived messages with the newest ones on top.

2. **Click the Compose Message icon that appears to the right of the inbox search bar.**

   It looks like a piece of paper with a pencil.

3. **Start typing the name of the person you're sending a message to.**

   LinkedIn automatically starts suggesting matches. Select the one you want from the drop-down menu.

4. **Compose your message in the box that says, "Click here to type your message," as shown in Figure 11-2.**

   Make sure you clearly identify yourself and the reason you are writing. Remember: Don't try to sell the recipient anything right away!

5. **Hover your mouse pointer over your name that is in bold print at the bottom of the message and click the pencil icon that appears.**

   A box opens in which you can add a signature. You have a total of 150 characters to work with when creating your signature. Use them wisely!

6. **Click the Send button when you're finished.**

   Now sit back and wait for a reply!

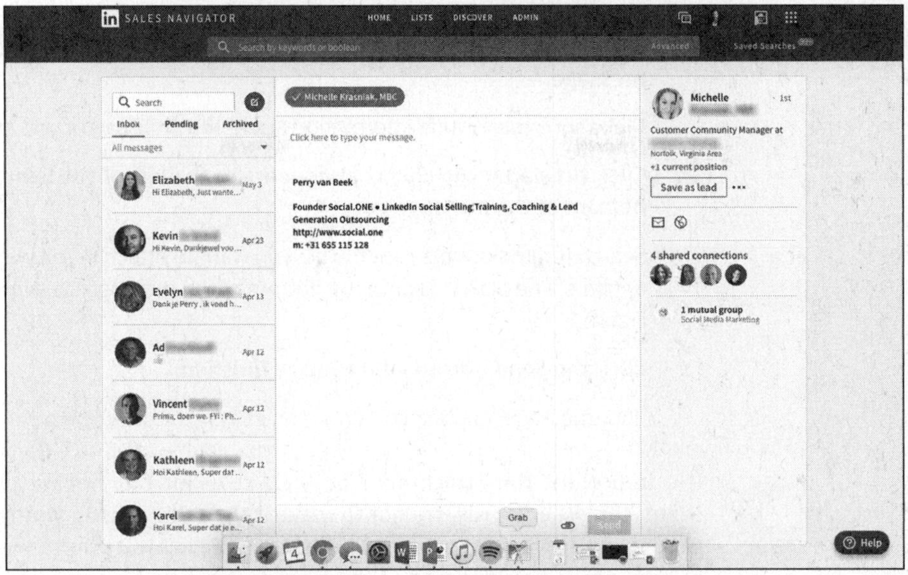

FIGURE 11-2:
Compose your
message here.

Adding Attachments to Your InMail Messages

Sales Navigator gives you the option of adding attachments to the InMail messages you send out, and you should take advantage of that opportunity as much as you can. Chances are, your company has some sales and marketing materials that it gives out to people at trade shows, conferences, and meetings with outside stakeholders. Why not include one or two of those documents in an InMail message you're sending to a prospect? It's easy to do so, just follow these steps:

1. **From your Sales Navigator home page, click the inbox icon in the main navigation bar at the top of your screen.**

   Your inbox home page opens. The default view is of your unarchived messages with the newest on top.

2. **Click the Compose Message icon that appears to the right of the inbox search bar.**

   It looks like a piece of paper with a pencil.

3. **Start typing the name of the person you're sending a message to.**

   LinkedIn automatically starts suggesting matches. Select the one you want from the drop-down menu.

4. **Compose your message in the box that says, "Click here to type your message."**

Make sure you include information about the attachment you are including.

5. **Click the paper clip icon that appears to the left of the Send button at the bottom of the message box.**

Search for and double-click the file you want to attach in the window that appears. The file loads onto the bottom of the message, as shown in Figure 11-3.

6. **Click the Send button when you're finished.**

Your message (and attachment) is on its way to the recipient!

TIP

It's important the attachment be both relevant but not necessarily the "main event." In other words, try not to make it the main reason you're writing. Instead, send it as supporting material to reinforce the subject you're writing about. Think of it this way. Could you send the message without the attachment, but including the attachment makes the message all the better? If the answer to that question is yes, by all means include it.

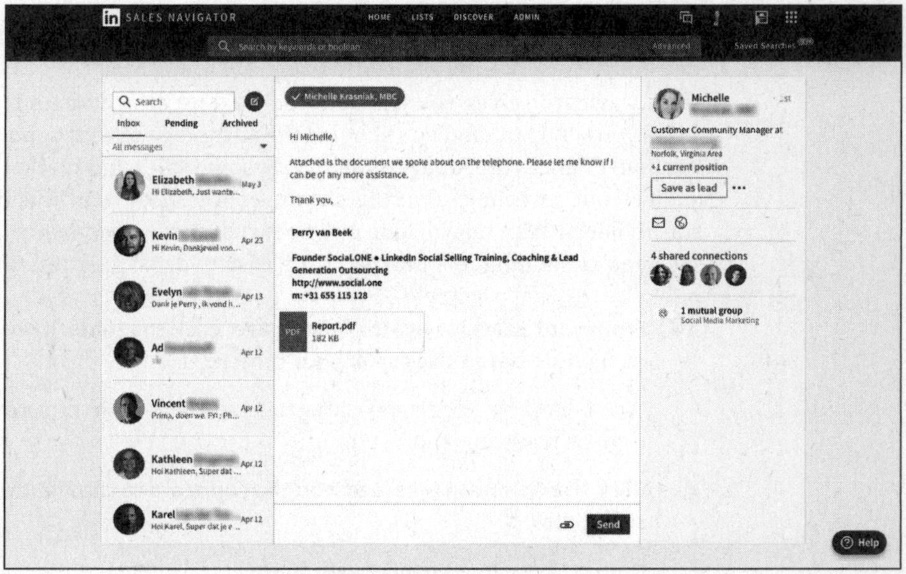

FIGURE 11-3:
Attaching a file to
a Sales Navigator
message.

That's not to say that you should be loading each InMail message up with every piece of documentation you think would be of interest to the recipient. Keep it to one or two attachments at a maximum, and make sure they're more informational than salesy.

REMEMBER

Keep cognizant of file size. Not everyone has a fast Internet connection. The last thing you want to do is send a massive file to a prospect and have it use up all of his or her data or worse — freeze up the prospect's computer!

TIP

If you have a Team-level or Enterprise-level Sales Navigator account, consider using PointDrive instead of including the attachment to your message. Using PointDrive, you gain valuable insights into how your content is consumed, and you can set certain parameters such as validity of the information or add a password. More on using PointDrive can be found in Chapter 7.

LinkedIn Sales Navigator for Gmail

If you use Gmail for your email client, Sales Navigator has a plug-in that integrates with Gmail to make your Sales Navigator experience even richer. Sales Navigator for Gmail shows you LinkedIn profile data for your contacts, leads, and prospective leads directly in Gmail. You can leverage that knowledge when you message them as well as save leads to Sales Navigator directly in your Gmail inbox.

You can get the plug-in here: https://business.linkedin.com/sales-solutions/compare-plans/sales-navigator-for-gmail. From this webpage, click the "Add to Gmail" button that appears in the middle of the page. The Google Chrome Web Store opens. Click the +Add to Chrome button that appears in the following screen. Once the extension is added, you will have a small Sales Navigator icon in the top right of your Chrome browser window.

Here's how it works: When you start to compose an InMail message to someone, that person's public LinkedIn profile details such as name, photo, current location, place of employment, and degree of connection becomes visible. If you're already first-degree connections with this person, you see additional information such as his or her phone number or website (if it is included on his or her profile).

IN THIS CHAPTER

» **Updating billing information**

» **Tracking InMail and messaging**

» **Turning on TeamLink**

» **Managing users**

» **Monitoring your usage reports**

Chapter **12**

Ten Tips for Account Management

U nderneath the hood of your LinkedIn Sales Navigator account is a section called Administrator Settings. This is where you do everything from upgrading your plan, cancelling your plan, and updating your payment information to connecting your company's customer relationship management (CRM) system. In this chapter, I take you through the most important settings to keep on top of to ensure Sales Navigator runs smoothly for you.

Accessing Administrator Settings

The Admin Settings page, shown in Figure 12-1, is where all the behind-the-scenes Sales Navigator settings and preferences are set and edited. To access the Admin Settings page, hover your mouse pointer over the Admin link in the main navigation bar at the top of your screen and select Admin Settings from the drop-down menu.

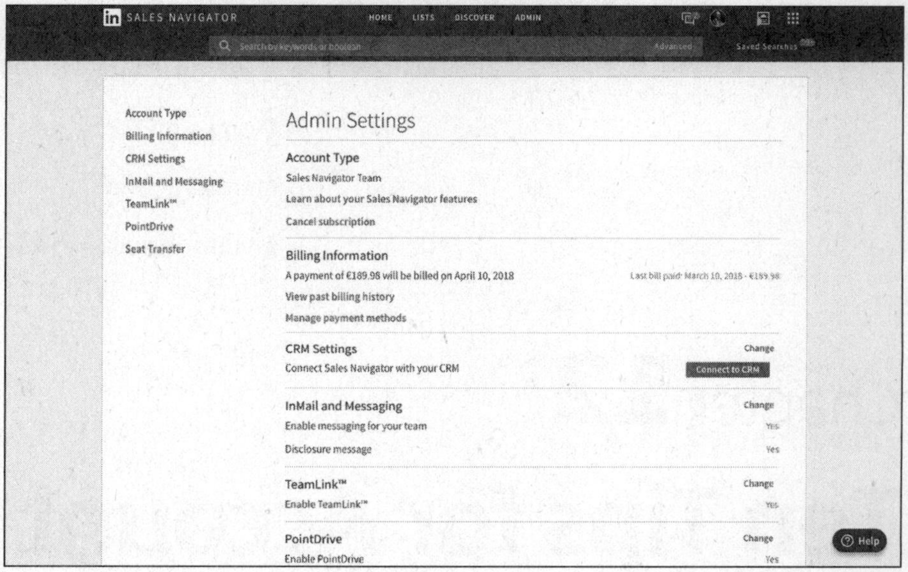

FIGURE 12-1:
The Admin
Settings page.

Once you're on the Admin Settings page, you'll see a menu of options on the left side of the page. Here is the information and settings you can access from this page, many of which I discuss in the following sections:

- >> Account Type
- >> Billing Information
- >> CRM Settings
- >> InMail and Messaging
- >> TeamLink
- >> PointDrive
- >> Seat Transfer

Viewing Account Types and Billing Information

The Account Type and Billing Information sections of the Admin Settings page are where you go when you want to learn more about the features offered by your specific Sales Navigator plan (Professional, Team, or Enterprise). Clicking the "Learn about your Sales Navigator features" link underneath Account Type takes you to the page shown in Figure 12-2. If you're thinking about upgrading to a Professional- or Team-level plan, this is also a handy place to visit to see the additional features you'll have access to by upgrading. The Account Type section is also where you can cancel your subscription. (But why would you want to?)

The Billing Information section underneath Account Type is where you can see your billing history and edit or delete your credit card information. It is good practice to take a look at your billing history (at least occasionally) to keep track of when your subscription renews and to keep a running tab on how much you've been spending on the service.

Connecting Sales Navigator to Your Company's CRM System

Chances are, your company has a customer relationship management (CRM) system. Sales Navigator integrates with some of the more popular systems — Salesforce, Microsoft Dynamics, and HubSpot — by matching people and company records with lead and account profiles and automatically importing them into the user's Saved or Suggested Leads pages.

This feature is helpful because you and your team don't have to reinvent the wheel and spend a lot of time either transferring over accounts from your CRM into Sales Navigator or search for leads and accounts individually.

Managing Access to InMail and Messaging

Sales Navigator allows you to send a set number of InMails per month (the number depends on your subscription level), so you may want to manage your team's ability to send InMails. Furthermore, if you want to limit the messaging capabilities of other members on your dashboard, the InMail and Messaging section on the Admin Settings page is the place to do that as well.

TIP

Limiting messaging is a good idea if, for example, you have new sales professionals on your team who may be in a probational period and you don't want them to have direct access to leads. On the other side of the coin, limiting messaging capabilities also ensures that disgruntled employees don't do (or say) anything that might put your company in a bad light.

Another setting in this section is the ability to turn on and off a disclosure message that is appended to the bottom of every message sent from your team account that gives the recipient the option to unsubscribe from receiving any more messages from you or other people on your company account. Figure 12-3 shows you an example of this kind of message.

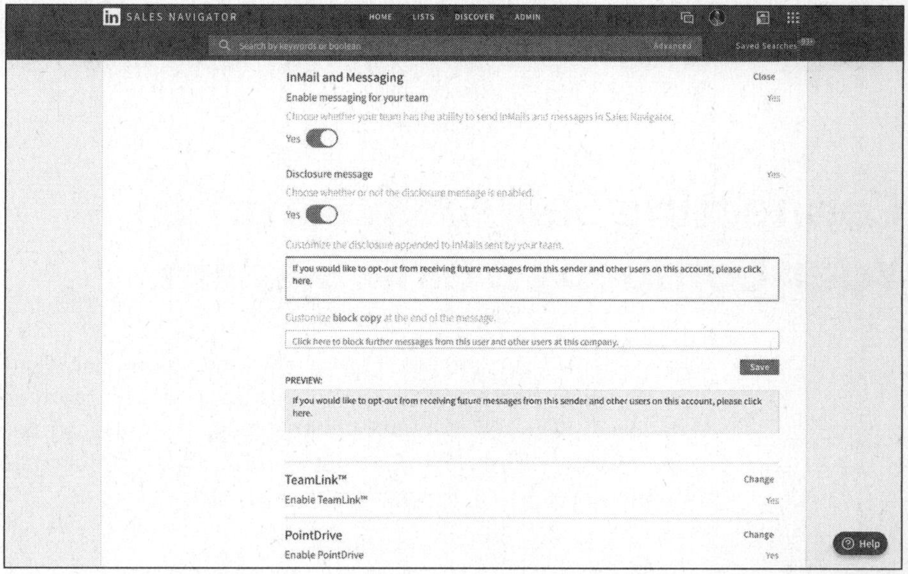

FIGURE 12-3: Recipients can opt-out from receiving messages from you in the future.

REMEMBER

The individuals doing the sending cannot see the message at the bottom, but the recipients can.

While you can toggle this disclosure setting on and off, I recommend you leave it on, as it shows the recipient that you have no interest in spamming them. Chances are, not every recipient will unsubscribe, but it's nice to have the option. LinkedIn is serious about keeping the network free from spam — and heavy-handed selling.

Enabling TeamLink

In Chapters 1 and 5, I discuss in great length the virtues of the TeamLink feature available in Team- or Enterprise-level Sales Navigator plans. To refresh your memory (or give you a brief introduction if you are one of those readers who likes to start at the end of a book and work backward), TeamLink is the ability for people on your Sales Navigator account to see and search each other's connections. This is a great way to expand your network and lead pool and opens up opportunities for warm leads to boot.

In the TeamLink section of the Admin Settings page you can toggle the TeamLink feature on or off. Needless to say, I highly recommend you leave this setting on! After all, you're on Sales Navigator (and LinkedIn in general) to grow your network, so why would you not take advantage of this option?

Activating New Users

When you need to add a new user to your Sales Navigator account, it's easy to do via email from the Seat Management screen. To access Seat Management, click the Admin link in the main navigation bar at the top of your screen and then select Seat Management from the drop-down menu. The Sales Navigator Seat Management dashboard opens, as shown in Figure 12-4.

At the top of the dashboard is a quick glance at your team status. In Figure 12-4 you see that there are three people on my account (myself and my associates, Alex and Marc); I have one open seat; all three of our seats are Active (meaning, we all completed the on-boarding process — the series of steps Sales Navigator took us through when we logged in for the first time); and finally, there are no seats awaiting activation. (Below the total seats number is the "Manage seats" link. Clicking that brings up a box where you can purchase more seats.)

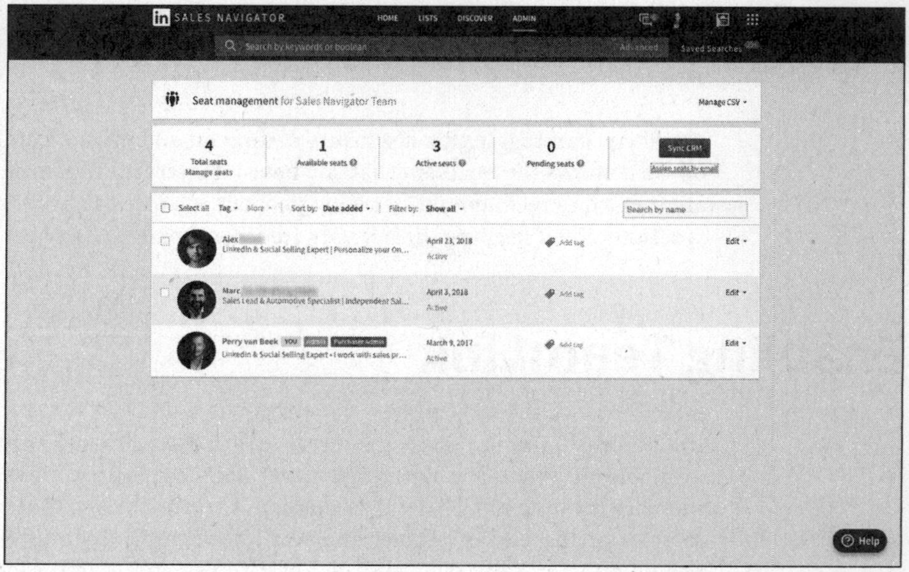

FIGURE 12-4:
This is where you manage all of the "seats" or accounts that fall under your Sales Navigator subscription.

On the far right of this dashboard status line is a link that, when clicked, lets you assign any available seats using a person's email address. This is helpful if you have a large number of seats to assign and you want to batch the process. You can add up to 200 email addresses address at a time. To assign an available seat, follow these steps:

1. **Navigate to the Seat Management home page by clicking the Admin link in the main navigation bar at the top of your screen and selecting Seat Management from the drop-down menu.**

   Your Seat Management dashboard opens.

2. **Click the "Assign seats by email" link that appears on the right side of the screen, underneath the Synch CRM button.**

   A screen that looks like the one shown in Figure 12-5 appears.

3. **Enter the email address of the person you want to invite in the left side of the box and click the "Add all" link.**

   That person's email address moves to the right side of the box. Do this for all the email addresses you want to add.

4. **Click the Assign button when you're finished adding all the email addresses of the people you want to invite.**

   These people are now added to your Seat Management dashboard. Each invitee's status is set to "Pending" until he or she completes the on-boarding process.

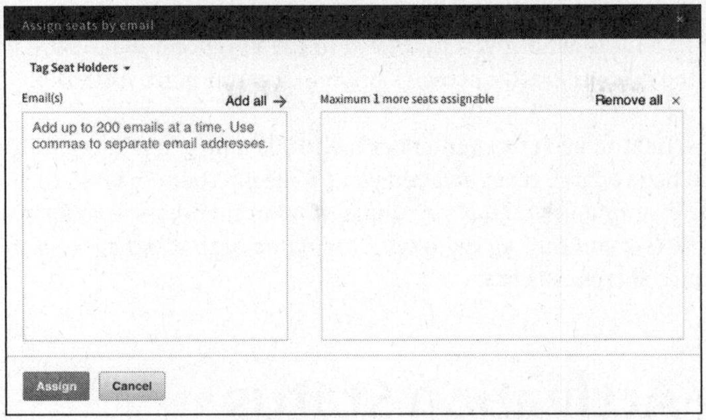

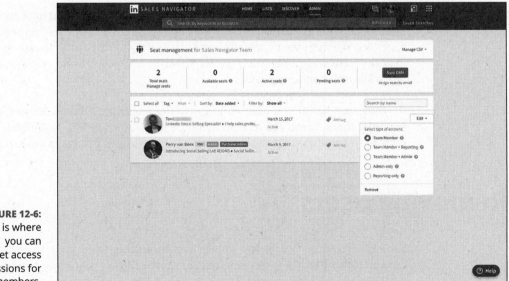

FIGURE 12-5:
Assign seats by email from this screen.

REMEMBER

Though you may be the administrator of the account, team members have access to all the same features you do except Seat Management and Usage Reporting.

The final section in the Seat Management dashboard is a button to sync your CRM. (I discuss how to connect your company's CRM earlier in this chapter.) To the right of each team member's entry is an Edit link that when clicked opens up the drop-down menu shown in Figure 12-6. This is where you control the different permissions the individual is given. For example, you may want members to have access to reporting capabilities but not the administrator settings. In that case, you'd click the Team Member + Reporting radio button to activate it.

FIGURE 12-6:
Here is where you can set access permissions for team members.

Be careful to whom you give keys to the kingdom! Make sure whoever has access to the administrative settings of your account is trustworthy.

Also next to each team member's entry is a link to add tags. Tags are handy when you have a large team and you want to group them in ways to assist with searches. For example, if you have a couple of team members who specialize in an obscure industry, you can tag them with the name of that industry so that finding them in future searches is easy.

Checking Activation Status and Sending Reminders

To ensure your team gets up and running on Sales Navigator as soon as possible, it's a good idea to keep an eye on who has accepted the invitation and completed the on-boarding process and who still has to do so. If you only have a handful of users on your Sales Navigator account, a quick glance at the top of your Seat Management page tells you how many active seats you have and how many are still pending. If you have pending seats, you can locate the individual by clicking the Filter By drop-down menu that appears at the top of the list of members and selecting the Pending option. This brings up all users who have not completed the on-boarding process yet.

It's a good idea to send a message to pending users to remind them of the importance of activating their Sales Navigator accounts. It's handy to send them a message directly from your LinkedIn account; therefore, they will already be logged into the network, making it easy for them to click over to Sales Navigator and begin the onboarding process.

On the other hand, you can remind pending users the "old-fashioned way" by emailing them directly to remind them. Or if you're *really* old-fashioned, you can pick up the phone and give them a call. (Do people still do that nowadays?)

Removing Users

Sometimes it's necessary to remove team members from your Sales Navigator account. Maybe they left the company, or maybe they've just moved on to another position and no longer need access to your Sales Navigator service. It's easy to remove individual seat holders from your dashboard, just follow these steps:

1. **Navigate to the Seat Management home page by clicking the Admin link in the main navigation bar at the top of your screen and selecting Seat Management from the drop-down menu.**

   Your Seat Management dashboard opens.

2. **Locate the user you want to remove from the list of active users.**

   The quickest way to find a particular user is by typing the person's name into the search box that appears in the top-right corner of the users list.

3. **Click the Edit link to the right of the user's name and select Remove from the drop-down menu.**

4. **Click the Continue button to confirm removal.**

   A message appears confirming the removal of the seat holder.

Viewing Usage Reports

If you have a Sales Navigator Team- or Enterprise-level account, you have access to the activity data of your team in the form of a usage report. Updated daily, the usage report is a great place to get a comprehensive overview of your entire Sales Navigator team account (see Figure 12-7).

To access the Usage Reporting page for your team, hover your mouse pointer over the Admin link in the main navigation bar at the top of your screen and select Usage Reports from the drop-down menu.

You should take a look at this page regularly to stay abreast of how your team is performing on Sales Navigator. A number of helpful charts show performance indicators such as the team's average Social Selling Index (SSI) score, the number of searches performed, and the number of InMails sent. To the right of each chart are each team member's individual scores.

Sales Navigator also gives you the option to filter the usage report to isolate data from a specific user, time frame, or tag. To filter, select the appropriate option from the Filter By drop-down menu located directly above the colorful SSI data charts.

Figure 12-7 shows the top part of the usage report, which includes the average team SSI score and a chart plotting your team's average score over the past 30 days. However, Sales Navigator gives you the option to filter that activity to isolate data from the last seven or 30 days, the last calendar year, or by the existing calendar year.

FIGURE 12-7:
Your team's SSI
information.

Scrolling down the usage report you see the charts shown in Figure 12-8. The top chart plots the number of daily active users on your account — the number of people on your team who have performed at least one action on Sales Navigator every day. The middle and bottom charts illustrate the number of leads and accounts saved, also within a one-month period. Scrolling even farther you see the number of searches performed by a user (on both LinkedIn and Sales Navigator), the number of profiles viewed, and finally, the number of InMail messages sent (see Figure 12-9).

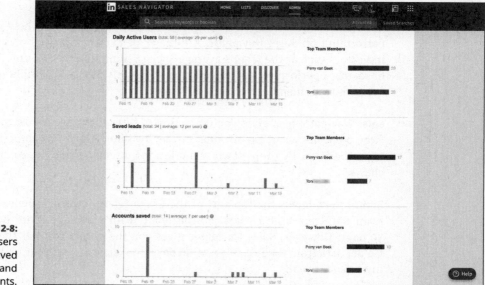

FIGURE 12-8:
Daily active users
as well as saved
leads and
accounts.

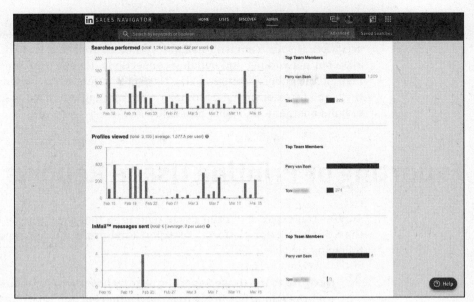

FIGURE 12-9:
Searches performed, profiles viewed, and InMails sent.

TIP

Because accounts get only a set number of InMails each month, keeping an eye on the InMails sent chart helps you stay on top of who is sending what and how many.

Finally, in Figure 12-10, you see the number of messages sent (non-InMail) as well as the number of unique connections across all users. Sales Navigator counts a unique connection as a first-degree connection, but this number is the aggregate of all connections made, even those made through TeamLink.

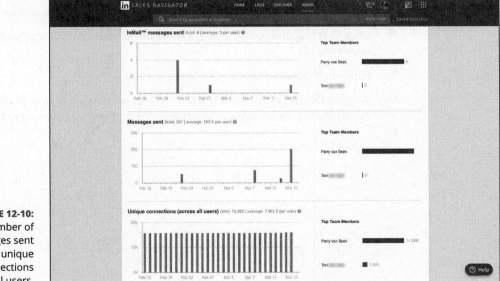

FIGURE 12-10:
The number of messages sent and unique connections across all users.

So why are the usage reports so important? For one, Sales Navigator is a paid sub-scription. If your team isn't using it, resources are being wasted. Social selling is all about networking and building connections. If your team isn't taking advan-tage of the robust features Sales Navigator offers social-selling professionals, they, and by extension your company, are missing out on so many opportunities to build a large — and quite possibility lucrative — network.

Exporting or Printing Usage Reports

Admins can export and print usage reports so that they can use them outside of the Sales Navigator platform. To export (and print) a usage report, perform the following steps:

1. **Navigate to the Usage Reporting page by hovering your mouse pointer over the Admin link in the main navigation bar and selecting Usage Reports from the drop-down menu.**

   The Usage Reporting page for your team appears.

2. **Filter the data using whatever criteria you choose.**

   Sales Navigator lets you filter by time frame, user, and tag.

3. **Click the "Download as CSV" link that appears in the top-right corner of the screen.**

   A message appears letting you know that your report is being generated. Once completed, another message appears at the top of the screen that says, "Your report was generated successfully," and includes a link to download the report.

4. **Click that link and navigate to the location on your computer where you saved the file.**

5. **(Optional) Double-click the CSV file to open it.**

6. **To print the file, either click the Ctrl + P keys on your keyboard or click File in the top menu bar and select Print from the drop-down menu.**

Chapter **13**

Ten Social-Selling Leaders to Follow

While I poured my blood, sweat, and tears into providing you with the best possible LinkedIn Sales Navigator and social-selling resource guide, one person and one book cannot give you every perspective of social selling. That's why I compiled this list of social-selling leaders I think you should follow. Trust me when I say that narrowing it down to just ten was extremely difficult! There are so many wonderful, talented, and helpful social-selling professionals out there who can offer additional perspectives and advice on how to succeed with social selling. In no particular order, here are my suggestions.

Melonie Dodaro

www.linkedin.com/in/meloniedodaro

Melonie Dodaro (Figure 13-1) is the author of *The LinkedIn Code* and the Chief Executive Officer of Top Dog Social Media. She and her team provide digital sales and marketing training, which includes a heavy emphasis on social selling, to professionals worldwide. Her latest book, *LinkedIn Unlocked,* is "a social-selling roadmap that will help you generate a consistent flow of quality leads."

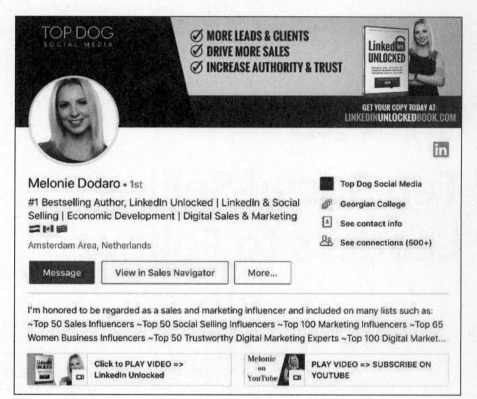

FIGURE 13-1:
Melonie Dodaro.

Jan Willem Alphenaar

www.linkedin.com/in/jwalphenaar

Jan Willem Alphenaar (Figure 13-2) is a LinkedIn sales trainer, keynote speaker, and the creator of the PEAS model for social selling on LinkedIn. He's made over 500 appearances and was a finalist for the best speech in the Netherlands in 2017. Some of the topics Jan Willem speaks about are social selling with LinkedIn and the effect online trends have on the customer experience.

FIGURE 13-2:
Jan Willem
Alphenaar.

Koka Sexton

www.linkedin.com/in/kokasexton

Koka Sexton (Figure 13-3) is the Senior Manager of Content and Editorial at Slack, the business platform that connects teams with the apps, services, and resources they need to collaborate and get things done. Prior to joining Slack, Koka was the founder of Social Selling Labs, which helped businesses and sales professionals "design, implement, and leverage social selling, content marketing, and social media applications like LinkedIn and others to build a sales pipeline."

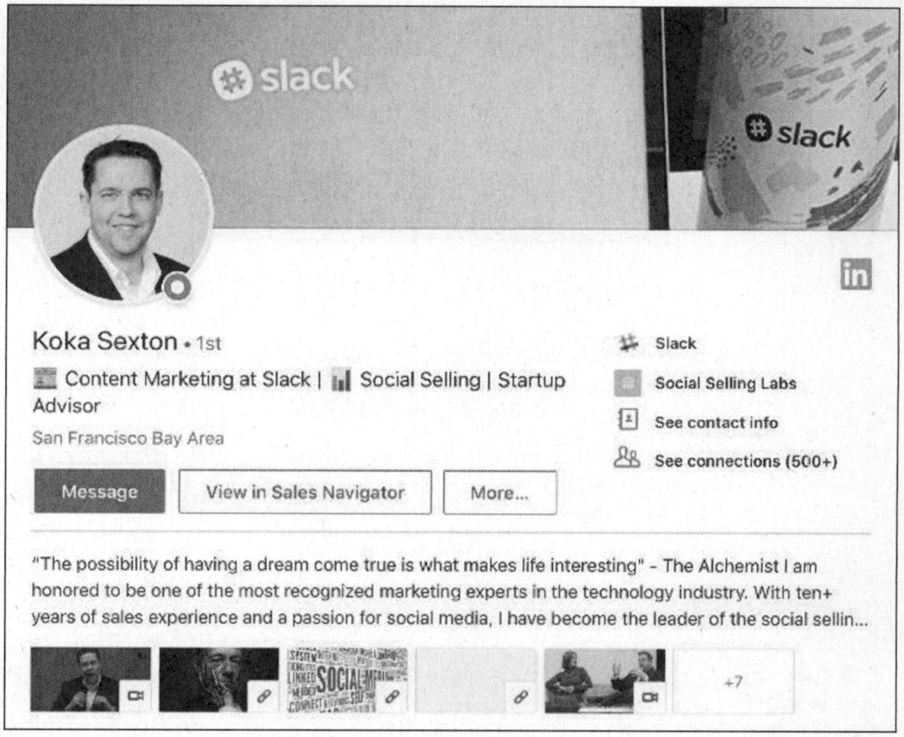

FIGURE 13-3:
Koka Sexton.

Neal Schaffer

www.linkedin.com/in/nealschaffer

For close to a decade, Neal Schaffer (Figure 13-4) has been a social media consultant and keynote speaker whose presentations include topics such as "The Evolution from Social Media to Social Business," "Social Selling: How to Leverage Social Media for B2B Sales," and "Maximizing LinkedIn for Business." He has spoken at more than 200 events all over the world including the popular Social Media Marketing World and Social Media Success Summit.

FIGURE 13-4:
Neal Schaffer.

Mic Adam

www.linkedin.com/in/micadam

Mic Adam (Figure 13-5) is a social-selling professional, social media policy maker, and trainer. He helps his clients increase sales by communicating and promoting each organization's unique value propositions for its products and services. He helps companies determine their return on investment for their social media activities by focusing on closing the gap between social media and business.

FIGURE 13-5:
Mic Adam.

Richard van der Blom

www.linkedin.com/in/richardvanderblom

Richard van der Blom (Figure 13-6) is a LinkedIn expert and social-selling trainer. He has over 15 years of experience in various sales roles and has trained more than 10,000 professionals at 400 companies the power of LinkedIn and social selling. He developed the B.E.S.T. Social Selling training system (Brand – Enlarge – Support – Transaction) to teach people how to quickly and easily find new clients using LinkedIn.

Alex Kroon

www.linkedin.com/in/alex-kroon

Alex Kroon (Figure 13-7) is a valuable member of my team here at Social.ONE. He is a LinkedIn expert and social-selling strategist who knows the power of communication and building relationships with prospects to build a rapport. Alex trains sales professionals on how to maximize their resources using LinkedIn for prospecting.

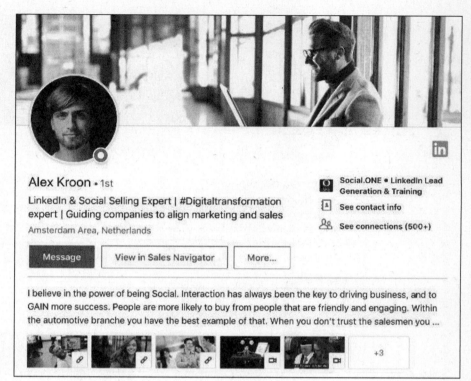

Mark Williams

www.linkedin.com/in/mrlinkedin

Mark Williams (Figure 13-8) is the founder of Winbusinessin, an online social-selling training and support business that provides help to small and medium-sized businesses. If you enjoy podcasts, I highly recommend you sign up for his weekly LinkedIn podcasts to hear valuable tips on using LinkedIn and social selling.

FIGURE 13-8:
Mark Williams.

Wendy van Gilst

www.linkedin.com/in/wendyvangilst

After attending the LinkedIn Road Show 2016 in London, Wendy van Gilst (Figure 13-9) realized a lot of people have similar challenges and questions about social selling. So she decided to set up the Social Selling Experts LinkedIn group. This LinkedIn group is an engaged group of people who are passionate about social selling and who are open to sharing experiences and learning from one another. If you are involved in social selling, make sure you join the Social Selling Experts Group on LinkedIn!

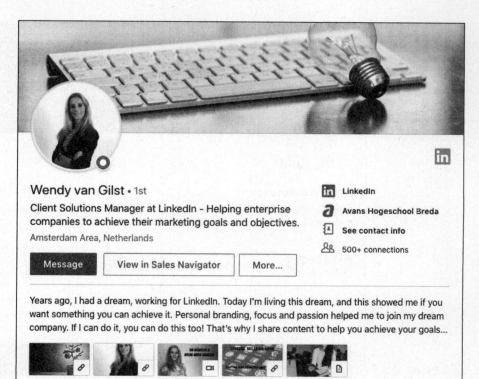

Wendy van Gilst • 1st

Client Solutions Manager at LinkedIn - Helping enterprise companies to achieve their marketing goals and objectives.

Amsterdam Area, Netherlands

[Message] [View in Sales Navigator] [More...]

LinkedIn

Avans Hogeschool Breda

See contact info

500+ connections

Years ago, I had a dream, working for LinkedIn. Today I'm living this dream, and this showed me if you want something you can achieve it. Personal branding, focus and passion helped me to join my dream company. If I can do it, you can do this too! That's why I share content to help you achieve your goals...

FIGURE 13-9:
Wendy van Gilst.

Gabe Villamizar

www.linkedin.com/in/gabevillamizar

Last but certainly not least, is Gabe Villamizar (Figure 13-10). Gabe is the head of B2B marketing at Lucid. He is recognized as a leading social-selling and social media practitioner by LinkedIn, *Forbes* magazine, *Huffington Post,* Forrester, and Salesforce. Gabe's social-selling online courses were recently published on Lynda. com and LinkedIn Learning, and have already been watched over 30,000 times.

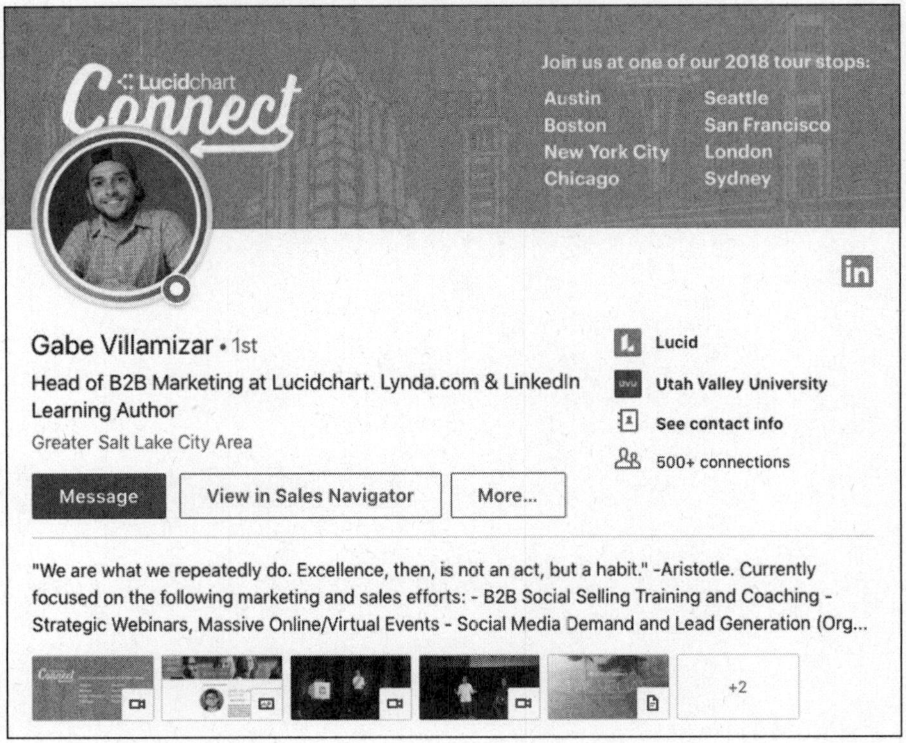

FIGURE 13-10: Gabe Villamizar.

Chapter **14**

Ten More Social-Selling Resources

I refer to many resources when I'm involved in my social-selling activities. This chapter lists my top ten favorites — I hope you find them just as useful as I do.

LinkedIn Profile Cheat Sheet

www.linkedincheatsheet.com

Before you start your social-selling journey with LinkedIn Sales Navigator, you need to make sure your LinkedIn profile is up to par. This simple-to-follow LinkedIn Profile Cheat Sheet walks you through optimizing your profile in 15 easy-to-follow steps (Figure 14-1).

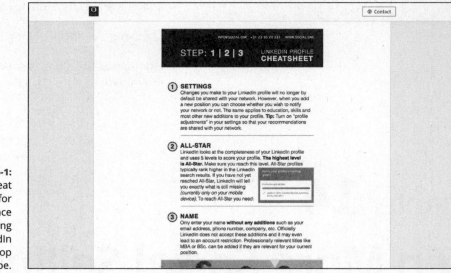

FIGURE 14-1:
Keep this cheat sheet on hand for a quick reference guide on getting your LinkedIn profile in top shape.

LinkedIn Unlocked

LinkedInUnlockedBook.com

The LinkedIn Profile Cheat Sheet is a quick fix. If you're looking to dive a lot deeper into LinkedIn and discover many of the secrets very few people know and use, you should read *LinkedIn Unlocked*, written by Melonie Dodaro, the Chief Executive Officer of Top Dog Social Media (Figure 14-2).

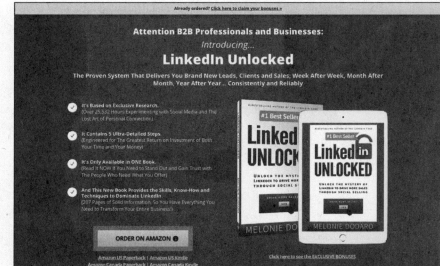

FIGURE 14-2:
LinkedIn *Unlocked* offers a comprehensive discussion of social selling on LinkedIn.

LinkedIn Sales Blog

`https://business.linkedin.com/sales-solutions/blog`

This is LinkedIn's own blog on anything related to business-to-business (B2B) sales and social selling (Figure 14-3). I highly recommend following it. It includes articles and posts from LinkedIn staff as well as from outside experts. It's become one of my go-to sources for everything LinkedIn.

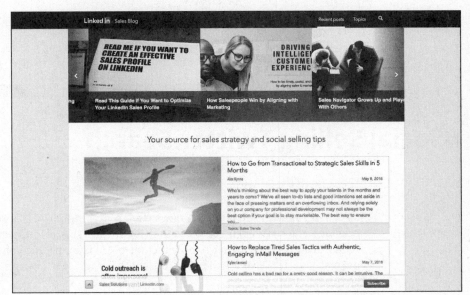

FIGURE 14-3: LinkedIn's sales blog is a one-stop shop for LinkedIn social-selling news.

Social Selling LinkedIn Search

`https://bit.ly/LinkedInSocialSellingSearch`

While you're navigating LinkedIn, why not search for *#SocialSelling* in the LinkedIn news feed? You will receive personal and customized search results that take into account who you're connected to or follow on LinkedIn (Figure 14-4). I recommend saving this page as a favorite in your Internet browser.

FIGURE 14-4:
Performing a search for *social selling* in LinkedIn returns a wealth of helpful information.

#Social Selling Twitter Search

```
https://bit.ly/TwitterSocialSellingSearch
```

Of course, as with the LinkedIn news feed, searching for *#SocialSelling* on Twitter provides you with even more results (Figure 14-5). I recommend filtering your search results even further to only include posts from people you follow or people nearest you. It's also a good idea to save this page as a favorite in your Internet browser.

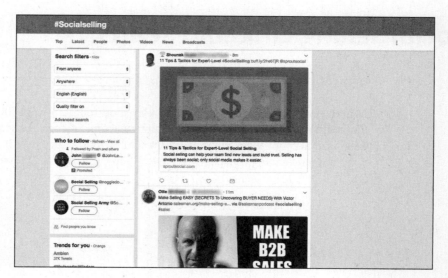

FIGURE 14-5:
Searching for "Social Selling" on Twitter is another great way to get the latest news.

Anders Pink

https://anderspink.com/briefing/4885/social-selling-latest-content-shared-by-25-gurus/1-month

This Anders Pink collection of social-selling articles is easily the best out there (Figure 14-6). This list contains some of the best golden nuggets about sales and social selling you will find.

FIGURE 14-6: Anders Pink is a top-notch source for social-selling information.

Top Dog Social Media

https://topdogsocialmedia.com/blog

Melonie Dodaro's blog on everything related to LinkedIn is a gold mine of information (Figure 14-7). It should be your go-to resource for advice on any challenges you may be having or for inspiration you may need regarding your social-selling activities on LinkedIn.

FIGURE 14-7:
The Top Dog
Social Media blog
is a site I refer to
regularly.

Venture Harbour

www.ventureharbour.com/20-insightful-lead-nurturing-statistics-charts

If you're one for statistics, I recommend you regularly check out Venture Harbour, a "digital innovation studio" that helps entrepreneurs and marketers grow their businesses. If you're still on the fence about social selling, Venture Harbour's list of 20 lead-nurturing statistics and charts should convince you to start today (Figure 14-8).

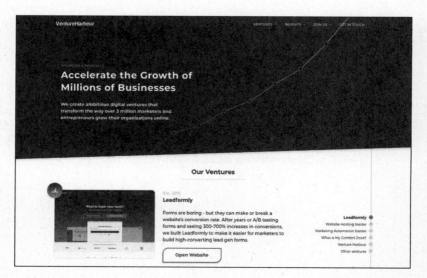

FIGURE 14-8:
Venture Harbour
will give you your
social-selling
statistics fix. (Try
saying that ten
times fast!)

HubSpot Sales Blog

`https://blog.hubspot.com/sales`

The HubSpot sales blog (Figure 14-9) is another general resource to keep an eye on when you're looking to stay up to date with everything that is happening in the world of social selling. I check this and the *Harvard Business Review* blog (discussed next) at least once a week to keep up with the latest news on B2B sales and social-selling news.

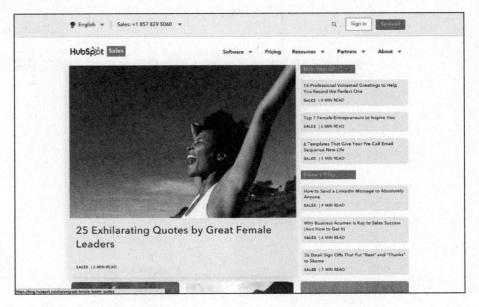

FIGURE 14-9:
The HubSpot blog provides helpful sales information.

Harvard Business Review

`https://hbr.org/topic/sales`

You're probably already familiar with the *Harvard Business Review* for your everyday business news, but did you know that it also offers a rich source of online information about sales and marketing? I have the *Harvard Business Review* Sales page bookmarked (Figure 14-10). It's one of the sites I make sure to check regularly.

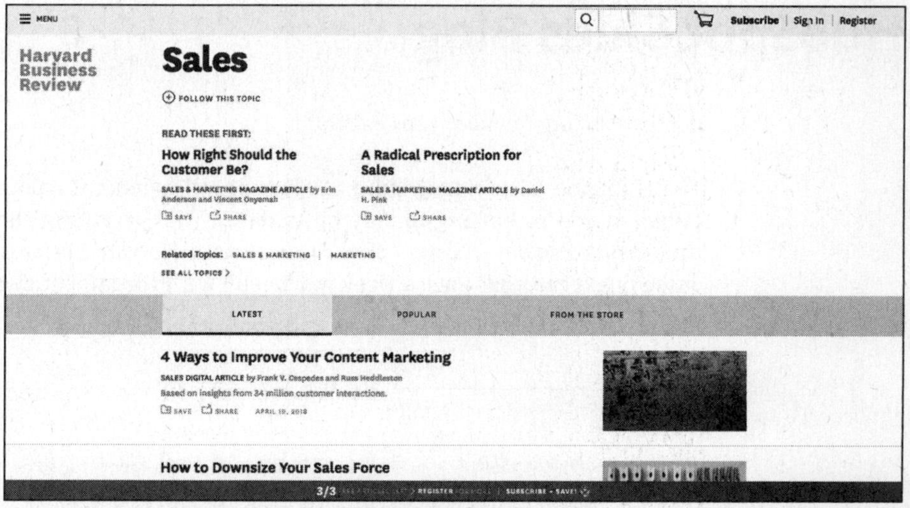

FIGURE 14-10:
The *Harvard Business Review* has sales-related information any social-selling professional would find helpful.

Index

F

families of employees, as stakeholders, 25
filtering updates
    by Account news, 101–102
    by Account shares, 102–103
    general discussion, 42–43
    by Job changes, 98–100
    by Lead news, 100
    by Lead shares, 101
    by most important, 43
    by most recent, 43
    by Sales alerts, 97–98
    by Suggested leads, 99–100
    by Top accounts, 44, 103
    by type, 43–44
    viewing similar and suggested leads, 82–83
focusing on right prospects
    defined, 8
    filtering searches by those who posted within
        past 30 days, 71–72
    likelihood of selling to existing clients vs. new
        clients, 33
    Social Selling Index dashboard, 15–16, 45
Franklin, Benjamin, 126

G

government entities, as stakeholders, 26

H

Harvard Business Review, 209–210
high-pressure tactics, 24
holistic approach to sales process, 31
HubSpot, 1, 28, 209

I

IBM, 1, 71
inbound marketing, 8
InMail feature
    accessing, 40
    adding attachments, 175–177
    archiving messages, 172

connecting with leads via, 120–121
    default signature, 174–175
    effective use of, 173
    inbox management, 132–134, 172–173
    limiting messaging, 182–183
    marking messages as unread, 172
    Pending tab, 172
    saving leads from inbox, 173
    searching, 173
    unread message indicator, 40
introduction requests, 114–115, 170–171

J

job changes
    congratulating for, 144
    filtering leads by, 153
    filtering updates by, 98–100
    searching by, 55
    viewing with mobile app, 143–144

K

Kroon, Alex, 197–198

L

Lead news filter, 100
Lead shares filter, 101
leads
    adding notes to, 79–80, 159–160
    adding tags to
        importance of, 79–80
        with mobile app, 158–160
        from profile page, 80–81
        from search results, 81–82
        suggestions for tags, 79
    advanced lead-generation tips
        conversation starters, 171–172
        increasing response rates and
            engagement, 169–170
        InMail, 172–177
        quantity versus quality, 167–168
        requesting introductions, 170–171

About the Author

Perry van Beek is a pioneer in social selling with LinkedIn. He founded Social.ONE and has been assisting companies with LinkedIn lead generation and social selling since 2009. Perry conducts trainings and presents keynotes at sales conferences throughout the world. Connect with him on LinkedIn at www.linkedin.com/in/perryvanbeek.

Perry spent the first 15 years of his career in international sales and already joined LinkedIn in 2004 as one of the first million users. He didn't discover the power for attracting new clients however, until he started his own export consulting business in 2007 and needed clients. He quickly fell in love with the opportunities LinkedIn offered people in B2B sales and started sharing all the tips and tricks he discovered with his network.

Because of that, he was invited to speak about LinkedIn at the end of 2009 for the first time. That's when he discovered how much he loved sharing his knowledge with others about the commercial opportunities that LinkedIn offers. So much so that he decided that this was going to be his new line of work. Barely three months later he was on national television in the Netherlands as *the* LinkedIn specialist. Since then he has been conducting in-house trainings and presenting keynotes at sales conferences throughout the world, from Europe to the United States to the Middle East.

Perry is now an in-demand keynote speaker speaking on the topics of LinkedIn and social selling at public events, client conferences, and sales conferences, including Harvard Business Review Poland in 2018.

His LinkedIn Profile Cheat Sheet (www.linkedincheatsheet.com) is a resource he's been sharing for free since 2010. It has just had its 14th revision. Visit Perry's website www.social.one for more social selling resources or his website devoted to his keynote speaking, www.perryvanbeek.com. You can contact Perry directly at perry@social.one.

Dedication

I wish to dedicate this book to the three most inspiring women in my life: my wife, Babette, and my sisters, Claire and Joyce. They continued to believe in me and supported me every step of the way. You're the best!

Author's Acknowledgments

Thank you to Amy Fandrei for initiating this project. Thank you to Michelle Krasniak and Katharine Dvorak from Wiley for staying on top of things and making this book possible. You did a truly fantastic job! Thanks also to Donna Serdula for being the Technical Editor.

A special thank you to my team, Marc van Domburg Scipio, Alex Kroon, and Ian Helgering who kept Social.ONE running smoothly while I concentrated on this book.

A big shout out to the business friends who've all supported me with this project and have now all very much become close personal friends: Rob de Graaf, Tonpeter Spaapen, Martijn Boomsma, Merlin Melles, Michael Kooitje, Bas Kiepe, Xander van Rijswijk, Otto Wijnen, Melonie Dodaro, and Maurice Jager.

And last but not least, of course a big shout out to all our clients who have entrusted us to co-create and guide them with their professional social-selling strategies.

Publisher's Acknowledgments

Senior Acquisitions Editor: Amy Fandrei

Content Editor: Michelle Krasniak

Project Editor: Katharine Dvorak

Technical Editor: Donna Serdula

Editorial Assistant: Matt Lowe

Production Editor: Mohammed Zafar Ali

Cover Image: © tridland / iStockphoto

PERSONAL ENRICHMENT

Staying Sharp dummies
9781119187790
USA $26.00
CAN $31.99
UK £19.99

Facebook dummies
9781119179030
USA $21.99
CAN $25.99
UK £16.99

Guitar dummies
9781119293354
USA $24.99
CAN $29.99
UK £17.99

Investing dummies
9781119293347
USA $22.99
CAN $27.99
UK £16.99

Beekeeping dummies
9781119310068
USA $22.99
CAN $27.99
UK £16.99

Digital Photography dummies
9781119235606
USA $24.99
CAN $29.99
UK £17.99

Meditation dummies
9781119251163
USA $24.99
CAN $29.99
UK £17.99

Pregnancy ALL-IN-ONE dummies
9781119235491
USA $26.99
CAN $31.99
UK £19.99

Samsung Galaxy S7 dummies
9781119279952
USA $24.99
CAN $29.99
UK £17.99

iPhone dummies
9781119283133
USA $24.99
CAN $29.99
UK £17.99

Crocheting dummies
9781119287117
USA $24.99
CAN $29.99
UK £16.99

Nutrition dummies
9781119130246
USA $22.99
CAN $27.99
UK £16.99

PROFESSIONAL DEVELOPMENT

Windows 10 dummies
9781119311041
USA $24.99
CAN $29.99
UK £17.99

AutoCAD dummies
9781119255796
USA $39.99
CAN $47.99
UK £27.99

Excel 2016 dummies
9781119293439
USA $26.99
CAN $31.99
UK £19.99

QuickBooks 2017 dummies
9781119281467
USA $26.99
CAN $31.99
UK £19.99

macOS Sierra dummies
9781119280651
USA $29.99
CAN $35.99
UK £21.99

LinkedIn dummies
9781119251132
USA $24.99
CAN $29.99
UK £17.99

Windows 10 ALL-IN-ONE dummies
9781119310563
USA $34.00
CAN $41.99
UK £24.99

SharePoint 2016 dummies
9781119181705
USA $29.99
CAN $35.99
UK £21.99

Fundamental Analysis dummies
9781119263593
USA $26.99
CAN $31.99
UK £19.99

Networking dummies
9781119257769
USA $29.99
CAN $35.99
UK £21.99

Office 2016 dummies
9781119293477
USA $26.99
CAN $31.99
UK £19.99

Office 365 dummies
9781119265313
USA $24.99
CAN $29.99
UK £17.99

Salesforce.com dummies
9781119239314
USA $29.99
CAN $35.99
UK £21.99

Coding dummies
9781119293323
USA $29.99
CAN $35.99
UK £21.99

dummies.com

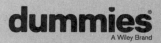
dummies
A Wiley Brand